PRAYERS FOR CATHOLIC MEN

MIKE PACER

Prayers for Catholic Men

Ignatius Edition

IGNATIUS PRESS SAN FRANCISCO

First edition published by Servant Books, 2008

Nihil Obstat: Rev. Ryan B. Browning, S.T.L.
January 6, 2025

Imprimatur: + David J. Malloy, D.D., J.C.L., S.T.D.
Bishop of Rockford, Illinois
January 7, 2025

Cover design by Chris Pelicano

ISBN 978-1-62164-739-3 (PB)
ISBN 978-1-64229-323-4 (eBook)
Library of Congress Control Number 2024950117
Printed in Slovenia

CONTENTS

PRAYERS FOR ANY TIME

PRAYERS FOR DISCERNMENT

FROM THE AUTHOR

Dear brother in Christ:

Your truest identity is that you are a beloved son of God. Your primary vocation is that which is proper to your particular state in life: son, perhaps husband, perhaps father.

I write this guide with the heartfelt desire to help you get to heaven and to bring those around you with you. It is aimed at bringing you peace—that elusive goal that we all desire in the midst of our hectic journey on earth.

Familiarize yourself with this guide and then use it throughout the day, every day. Carry it with you everywhere. Bring it with you in your car, into your school, into your office, and into your home.

Do not leave God at church. Bring him with you everywhere you go. Make Jesus personal to you—the Lord of your time, relationships, work, leisure, and treasures.

—Mike Pacer

THE SIGN OF THE CROSS

In the name of the Father
and of the Son
and of the Holy Spirit. Amen.

It is good to begin and end every prayer with the Sign of the Cross—not a perfunctory, habitual Sign of the Cross that looks more like swishing a fly away but a thoughtful and deliberate one.

By signing yourself with the cross, you are affirming your belief in the Triune God, recalling the crucifixion of your Savior Jesus Christ, identifying yourself as a Christian, and requesting the blessings of the Father, Son, and Holy Spirit.

From the early days of the Church, believers used this sign to show that they belonged to Christ and believed in all that he revealed. "At every forward step and movement," wrote the Church Father Tertullian, "at every going in and out, when we put on our clothes and shoes, when we bathe, when we sit at table, when we light the lamps, on couch, on seat, in all the ordinary actions of daily life, we trace upon the forehead the sign."

Practically, the Sign of the Cross is a physical cue, reminding you that you are about to do something very special and important: you are about to address your Lord God!

PRAYERS FOR EVERY DAY

God wants to be with you all the time. Turn to him throughout your day—from start to finish!

Trust in him at all times, O people;
pour out your heart before him;
God is a refuge for us.

PSALM 62:8

STARTING THE DAY

Every day when you wake up, you are faced with a choice: Are you willing to be the man God wants you to be? The moment the alarm sounds is the heroic moment. It is the moment that sets the tone for your entire day. You can shake off slumber, dedicate yourself to God, and get about the work of sanctifying yourself through your daily endeavors. Or you can succumb to laziness, hit the snooze button, and wait till later to drag yourself out of bed.

Get up, man! Say a prayer dedicating yourself and your day to your Lord and Creator. Embrace the day, with its joys and heartaches, successes and failures.

O my God,
I offer up my day to you.
I offer you my joys, my sorrows,
my sufferings, my accomplishments; anything that
I am or have.
I ask your help in everything I must do.
I especially ask your help in avoiding sin.
Mary my mother, Joseph my father,
my guardian angel, intercede for me.

CONFRONTING FEAR OF THE DAY

There are many causes for morning anxiety: work stress, family issues, financial difficulties, fear of the unknown—the list goes on. It is not unmanly to admit fear. A man acknowledges it and seeks to work through it.

Many fears do not dissipate immediately but must be borne for a period of time. This is a great opportunity for grace. It is an opportunity to offer up the pain of anxiety as a prayer for your family. It is also an opportunity to place your trust in God, even when that is not easy.

Lord Jesus, as true man you are intimately acquainted with fear.
In the Garden of Gethsemane, you agonized over your impending Passion and death
to the point that your sweat became like drops of blood.
Yet even then you said to your Father: "Thy will, not mine, be done."
I wish to imitate your loving example—
to accept this cross before me obediently.
I offer up this fear to you.
I unite my pain to that which you experienced,
for the good of my family and the salvation of their souls.
I trust that you will give me the strength I need.

Or:

Lord, if it be your will, take this fear from me.
Otherwise, help me to endure it as a prayer for my family and loved ones.

LUNCHTIME

Your day is half over. How has it gone? Have you worked hard? Have you been honest? Have you been charitable to those with whom you have come in contact?

Take a moment to refocus your day. God wants to be the Lord of your work as well as of your prayer. Maybe you have lost sight of him during the past several hours. Turn back to him now.

Lord Jesus, you labored in obscurity for much
of your life.
If you, who are Lord and God, saw fit to
sanctify yourself through ordinary work,
I must also recognize the supernatural value
of even my most mundane task.
Accept my work, performed honestly and
humbly,
as my ongoing prayer to you for the needs
of my family and those I love.
Strengthen me to see this workday to its
worthy conclusion.
Saint Joseph the Worker, intercede for me.

Please note: The traditional prayer of the Catholic Church for noon is the Angelus; between Easter and the Feast of Pentecost, the Regina Coeli is substituted. These prayers can be found in the Devotions and Miscellaneous Prayers chapter of this book.

HOME FROM WORK: HUSBANDS AND FATHERS

You have completed your workday. Perhaps this was a day of joy and success, perhaps one of great trial and suffering. Either way, you are about to enter into the domain of your primary vocation—that of husband and/or father.

Your wife and children have had their own joys and sorrows today. As difficult as it may be, endeavor to set aside any anger or sorrow you carry from the day. Do not make your home the outlet for your frustration.

If your day was wonderful, you may need to temper your enthusiasm in order to console your wife or children. Pause for a moment to pray before you walk into the house, focusing on the love you have for your family.

Loving Father, help me let go of the concerns of my work.
Tomorrow you will give me the necessary grace to confront the lingering challenges.
I release my anger and anxiety as a prayer for the consolation of my family.
Give me an attentive ear for my wife and children as they share their day.

Give me a loving heart to share in their joys and ease their sorrows.
Give me patience and wisdom to address their needs.
As I walk into my house, may I be a calming force and a source of strength.

DAILY SPOUSAL PRAYER

It is difficult to pray with your spouse every day. Some days you may not even feel like speaking to her. But you and your wife have vowed before God to love each other in good times and in bad. It is imperative that you work together to get to heaven.

You are responsible for your wife's soul and she for yours. Do you wish to please God? Then pray with your wife. He greatly desires this of you. And like all graces God gives, your little effort will be rewarded a thousandfold.

Lord Jesus, we place our marriage in your hands.
Help us grow in our love for you and for each other.
Grant us humility in recognizing and appreciating each other's strengths,
patience in accepting each other's weaknesses,

and understanding of each other's differences.
We thank you for the joys you have given us
and offer up to you the sorrows we have experienced.
May we always work together to reach our eternal happiness with you.

HOME FROM WORK: SINGLE MEN

You have completed your workday. Perhaps this was a day of joy and success; perhaps it was a day of great trial and suffering. Either way, the day is not over, and you must not lower your spiritual guard.

You may be tempted to celebrate your joys or drown your sorrows at a bar, vegetate in front of a television set or computer screen, or vent frustrations with friends or family members. Think instead of what you can do to know, love, and serve God with the rest of your day.

There are great spiritual books to read and inspiring movies to watch. There are many lonely people who would appreciate the occasional visit or phone call. There are all sorts of Church and community organizations in which to become involved (including men's faith groups and Bible study groups). And any time is a good time to read the Bible, pray, or "just talk to God".

Pause for a moment to pray as you walk into your house.

Loving Father, help me let go of the concerns of
my work.
Tomorrow you will give me the necessary grace
to confront the lingering challenges.
I release my anger and anxiety as a prayer for
the consolation of my family and friends.
My day is not over, and I wish to give the
remaining time to you.
Holy Spirit, guide me until I sleep.
Help me treat those with whom I come in contact
charitably.
Make the rest of my day a journey toward
heaven.

FOR A SINGLE MAN IN A SERIOUS RELATIONSHIP

Any woman you date is a beloved daughter of God and must be treated with great respect and dignity. As your relationship becomes more serious, it is imperative that you not become more "comfortable", for that usually means "lazy". Such an attitude will lead to taking this beautiful woman for granted or to a sexual intimacy that should be reserved for sacramental marriage.

Every day you must thank God for placing this woman in your life. Every day you must seek God's guidance about what he wants for this relationship.

Father, thank you for allowing _____ to come into my life.
I offer up our relationship to you for whatever you wish it to be.
Help me always recognize your beauty in her and treat her with love and respect.
Holy Spirit, enlighten both of us to know your divine will.
Strengthen us against temptations,
and help us make appropriate choices in our lives.
Mary, intercede for me to our Lord,
that I might always treat _____ with the same dignity I owe you
as the Blessed Mother of my Lord.

DAILY EXAMINATION OF CONSCIENCE

At the end of each day, it is important to examine your conscience for a few moments. Recall the events of your day. Identify your spiritual failings.

Make sure you address your primary weakness: maybe it is pride, anger, or laziness.

There is no reason to be embarrassed by your failings or to become despondent. You are human and therefore weak by nature. Your strength comes from honesty with God and with yourself.

Express true contrition for your faults. Resolve to struggle against them. Then be at peace. Tomorrow you will begin again, and God will give you his graces to move forward.

Begin by praying (with Peter in John 21:17):

Lord, you know all things. You know that I love you.

Consider each of the following:

Charity

- Did I treat my family and others with patience and respect?
- Was I cheerful?
- Did I avoid gossip?
- Did I humble myself and help others shine?

Work or Studies

- How did I use my time?
- Was I honest?
- Was my work an act of love for God?

Purity

- Did I avoid inappropriate visual images and conversations?
- If I am married, did my actions and thoughts support my daily goal of growing in love and respect for my wife?
- If you are not married: Did I respect the women I encountered as daughters of God?

Prayer

- Did I keep in touch with God throughout the day?

End by praying, *Jesus, forgive me and strengthen me*, or pray the Act of Contrition, found in The Sacrament of Reconciliation chapter of this book, page 128.

Please note: If you truly wish to grow in holiness, keep an inventory of your sins to bring with you when you next go to confession. Receive the Sacrament of Reconciliation regularly, at least once a month.

NIGHT PRAYER

Before drifting off to sleep, say good night to your heavenly Father, who has given you everything you have. He blesses you with all of your joys and successes and bears all of your pains with you. Try to give him your last conscious thought, and rest in his divine mercy and peace.

Father, I can do no more today.
I release all of my anxieties and burdens to you.
I know that you love me.
I entrust myself and all whom I love to the Sacred Heart of Jesus.
Grant me a restful sleep.

FOR ACCEPTING GOD'S LOVE AND FORGIVENESS

The lie within our mind is that we are never good enough and that we cannot be forgiven for our failings. We judge ourselves not by who we truly are, but by what we have done or failed to do.

You are God's beloved son. You are beautiful in his eyes. God loves you just as you are. While he wants you to endeavor to avoid sin and love him, this is not a condition for God's love, but your response to God's preexisting, eternal love for you.

Stop comparing yourselves to others. Stop worrying how others might see you. Stop trying to prove yourself to God. Just accept God's love. Moreover, if God loves you just as you are, you should love yourself as well. You are created in the very image and likeness of God. You are awesome!

My Father,
you created me in your image and likeness.
I am your son,
and you love me intimately and infinitely.
I accept your love.
I accept the fact that I am good,
possessing many good qualities
and reflecting your goodness.

Or:

My Father,
I choose to accept the truth that I am good and loved by you, just as I am!

PRAYERS FOR ANY TIME

In his first letter to the Thessalonians, Saint Paul admonishes us to "pray constantly" (1 Thess 5:17). Obviously, we cannot turn every conscious thought throughout an entire day to God. What we can do is to frame our day in prayer, support our day with prayer, and then let all of our regular daily activities be prayer.

Every activity—even the most mundane—done well and in love is prayer. We pray when comforting a grieving friend. We pray when we work hard to support our family. We pray when we take out the trash without complaining. But to remind ourselves that this is prayer and to keep ourselves focused on noble and good actions, we must feed out activities with prayer. We start our day with prayer. We end our day with prayer. And, as time permits, we return to prayer at various times throughout every day.

PRAYERS BASED ON THE THEOLOGICAL VIRTUES

Faith, hope, and love are referred to as the "theological virtues". They are infused into our souls in order to dispose us to live in relationship with God. For this reason, they are the keys to living a happy and holy life. God gives these virtues to us but does not make us accept them, embrace them, or seek to grow in them. If you want to grow in holiness, pray for these virtues regularly.

Act of Faith

O my God,
I believe that you are one God in three
divine Persons,
Father, Son, and Holy Spirit.
I believe that you created me in love,
to live in love with you now and for eternity.
I believe that you sent the Son
to save me from the effects of the original sin
of Adam
and from my own personal sins.
I believe that Jesus Christ is truly God and
truly man.
I believe that the Holy Spirit sanctifies and
guides the Church

and preserves its teachings from error.
I believe in these and all truths taught by the Holy Catholic Church.

Or:

Father, in love you have created me for you!
Jesus, in love you have saved me for you!
Holy Spirit, in love transform me for you!

Act of Hope

O my God, relying on your almighty power and infinite divine mercy,
I hope to obtain pardon of my sins and life everlasting,
through the merits of Jesus Christ, my Lord and Savior.

Or:

Lord, I hope to live with you forever!

Act of Love

Lord, you know all things;
you know that I love you.
Help me to love you with all of my heart,
with all of my mind,

with all of my soul,
and with all of my strength.
And because of my love for you,
may I love my neighbor as myself.

Or:

My Lord! My Love! My Life!

Simple "Acts of Love"

It is impossible for us to perform heroic acts of love for God and his children constantly, and we do not need to. Rather, we should focus on doing little acts of love on a regular basis. These are the true signs of the love in our heart. These are the surest path to heaven.

Simple acts of love include emptying the dishwasher, picking up a piece of trash in a public place, or cleaning out the gunk in the office sink without anyone knowing it. They include not complaining when someone cuts in front of you and purposely smiling while walking in a public place. One of the greatest acts of love is simply to listen to someone else. No accolades. No recognition. No "Look how good I am." Just a simple act of love.

Praise and thanksgiving are the most ignored forms of prayer, yet they are the most powerful.

What is the impetus for your reaching out to God in prayer at any given moment? If your answer is "to ask for something for myself or another", you would be giving what is probably the honest answer for almost all of us. It is a sad reality that we often ignore God when everything is going all right. But when we need something, then we start knocking on the door.

How often do you thank God for all of the wonderful things in this world? For your life? Your family? The roof over your head? How often do you allow yourself to marvel at the unfathomable awesomeness of God in creating all things and to praise him for the beauty of creation, the beauty of life, the beauty of loving relationships? How often do you praise God for being God?

Prayers of praise and thanksgiving foster an attitude of gratitude and a sense of awe and joy and instill in us a better understanding of God. Prayers of praise and thanksgiving lift us up from our feelings of fear and anxiety. They remind us of the good that exists in the midst of the bad. They lift our spirits. They help our souls soar to the heights of heaven.

FORMAL PRAYER OF PRAISE

You, Lord God, are the only God.
You are Three in One—Father, Son, and
Holy Spirit.
You created all things in heaven and earth
and are king over all.
You are holy,
and all your works are holy and wonderful.
You are almighty and powerful.
You are great and strong.
You are love.
You are goodness.
You are wisdom.
You are beauty.
You are glory.
You are humility.
You are gentleness.
You are faithfulness.
You are rest.
You are peace.
You are joy and gladness.
You are justice and mercy.
You are my guardian and defender.

You are my faith and consolation.
You are my courage and hope.
You are my life and salvation.
You are my beginning and end.
Amen.

INSPIRED BY A PRAYER OF
SAINT FRANCIS OF ASSISI

Formal Prayer of Thanksgiving

Thank you, Lord Jesus Christ,
for all the benefits and blessings that you have given me,
for all the pains and insults that you have borne for me.
Merciful Friend, Brother and Redeemer,
may I know you more clearly,
love you more dearly,
and follow you more nearly,
day by day.
Amen.

SAINT RICHARD OF CHICHESTER

Simple Prayers of Praise from the Heart

Any words of praise from the heart are great. Here are just some examples.

I praise you, Lord, for the sun, the moon, and the stars!

I praise you for your awesome plan of salvation!

I praise you for the beauty of my wife!

I praise you for my wonderful children!

I praise you for your great love for mankind!

Prayer of Thanksgiving by a Husband and Father

Lord, I always come to you when I want something.
But now I come before you and ask for nothing,
because you have given me everything.
Thank you for my life.
Thank you for my wife.
Thank you for my children.
Thank you for the roof over our heads and the food in our kitchen.
Thank you for our health and for our happiness.
Thank you for our family and our friends.
Thank you for the earth, the sky, the moon, and the stars.
Thank you for the wind and the waves.

Thank you for the birds and the beasts.
But most of all, thank you for you.

Prayer of Thanksgiving by a Single Man

Lord, I always come to you when I want something.
But now I come before you and ask for nothing,
because you have given me everything.
Thank you for my life.
Thank you for the roof over my head and the food in my kitchen.
Thank you for my health and for my happiness.
Thank you for my family and my friends.
Thank you for the earth, the sky, the moon, and the stars.
Thank you for the wind and the waves.
Thank you for the birds and the beasts.
But most of all, thank you for you.

Simple Prayers of Thanksgiving from the Heart

Any "thank you" from the heart is great. Here are some examples.

Thank you, Lord, for life.

Thank you for my wife and children.

Thank you for making me.

Thank you for loving me.

PRAYERS FOR MEALS

Whether alone or with your family, in your home or in public, always thank God for your meals. Everything is created by and a gift from God. What could be a better opportunity to acknowledge this truth than ingesting the food that sustains your very life? And when done in public, this is a great witness to your faith.

Before Meals

Bless us, O Lord,
and these thy gifts,
which we are about to receive from thy
bounty,
through Christ our Lord. Amen.

After Meals

We give you thanks, almighty God,
for these and all your gifts,
which we have received through Christ
our Lord. Amen.

There is no need to constantly say long "rote" or "flowery" prayers throughout the day. "Spontaneous prayers"—simple short prayers that turn the mind and heart to God—are sufficient. They can be said silently anywhere at any time throughout the day. In an instant, we are brought into the presence of God. We acknowledge God. We praise him. We thank him. We give ourselves to him.

Jesus, Mary, and Joseph, I give you my heart and my soul.

Lord, now it is not I who live but you who live in me.

Jesus, I trust in you!

Jesus, I hope in you!

Lord, you know all things; you know that I love you.

Lord, I believe; help my unbelief.

My Lord and my God!

Jesus, meek and humble of heart, make my heart like unto thine!

Lord Jesus, Son of the living God, have mercy on me, a sinner.

Lord, help me to decrease so that you may increase.

PRAYERS FOR DISCERNMENT

"Discernment" is not mere "problem solving". Nor is it merely a method of deriving an answer to a specific question. Discernment is the ability to judge well. In the spiritual context, it is the means by which we seek to align ourselves with God's will. Our Father created us in love. He wants nothing but the very best for us. Since he alone knows what that is, if we seek to be the most joyful and fulfilled we can be, we must seek to see our path forward as God sees it.

GENERAL PRAYER FOR DISCERNMENT

Lord, you created me for a purpose:
to be fully your beloved son and to be fully "me".
I want to be the beautiful son you see when you look at me.
I want to be the man you know I can be.
I want to walk closely with you down my particular path of life.
I want to make good decisions.
Show me the way.

We have been trained to determine an answer to a question in a certain way. We research; we analyze the data; we make a decision. Decision-making is then all about activity on our part. This is not so with discernment. In discernment, there are two necessary additional steps: we must ask God, and we must listen for his answer.

Prayer is a dialogue. Silence is the time when, after asking God for something, we listen for his response. Theoretically, this silence can be achieved anywhere at any time. Practically, we should find a quiet place of solitude (a church or adoration chapel is best). We might say a prayer of acknowledgement of God's presence and/or perhaps take a few deep breaths while calling to mind the fact that God is present. Ask the question and then just listen quietly for an answer.

Prayer Before Meditation

My Lord and my God, I firmly believe that you are here;
that you see me, that you hear me.
I adore you with profound reverence
and ask the grace to make this time of prayer fruitful.

My immaculate mother, Saint Joseph my father
and lord,
my guardian angel, intercede for me.

BASED ON A PRAYER BY
SAINT JOSEMARÍA ESCRIVÁ

Prayer When God Does Not Seem to Answer

We must not be discouraged when we do not receive an obvious answer to our prayers for discernment. We must be patient and ask again—and again. And we must patiently wait for an answer. That having been said, there are times that we determine that some action must be taken. In this case, make a decision and say the following prayer.

Father,
I don't know what you want me to do,
but I must do something.
I will _____.
Stop me if that is not what you want.

After saying this prayer, move forward. Our Lord loves this prayer for its honesty, humility, trust, and obedience. Either he will bless your decision or he will stop you and make another path known.

PRAYERS FOR DISCERNMENT OF VOCATION

As Christians, we acknowledge God's gift to us of free will and the ability to choose how we will live our life. However, we also recognize that God has a unique plan for each of us—a path of service of him, his Church, and his other children—that will best fulfill us and glorify him. When we speak of "discernment of vocation", we are referring to a process by which we determine to what state of life God is calling us.

Generally there are four states of life: (1) the priesthood, (2) the married life, (3) the religious life (for example, as a monk, brother, or consecrated layman), and (4) the celibate single life. In your discernment of God's call, none of them should be seen as a mere "fallback position". Rather, a man must be convinced that he is being specifically *called* to such a life. Otherwise, he should remain open to all possibilities until God makes his path clear. It must also be remembered that only the priesthood, religious life, and married life are necessarily permanent. It may be that God is calling a man to be single for a period of time before he calls him to a different state.

Every single male should pray this prayer. God does not simply call a few sinless "holy rollers" or "church nerds" to the priesthood. Even though the call is extraordinary, the Lord calls ordinary men—men who would make great husbands, men who have the gifts to be very successful in the working world.

However, God is not in the habit of sending down angels bearing golden invitations to the seminary. To receive the gift of priesthood, men need to be actively open to it, which means remaining quiet enough to hear it. Of course, the fact that you are a faithful Catholic with a prayer life alone does not mean that you are called to be a priest—no matter what the grandmothers at your parish might say. Still, who knows? God may be inviting you. He may be offering you this beautiful life—a life of unfathomable worth and fulfillment. Do you have the courage at least to ask? You have nothing to lose—and perhaps everything to gain.

Lord, I barely know how to ask if you desire me
to be a priest.
I am not worthy to be the instrument
by which you bring down your Body and Blood
for your people to receive.

I am not worthy to be the one by whom you baptize, forgive sins,
witness the bond of matrimony, anoint the sick, or bury the dead.
How could a sinner like me lead, teach, and comfort your people?
How could I be a father to an entire flock?
But how can I say no to you?
If you are calling me to be a priest, is this not where I will find true happiness?
Speak to me, Lord!
If this is what you want, if this is what will truly fulfill me,
then convict me of the joy that will come through this life,
and give me the strength to say yes.
If it is not what you want, if you have other plans for me,
then help me to be patient in hearing your will.

If you think you might be called to be a priest, talk about it with your pastor, with the director of vocations of your diocese (or of a religious order), or with any priest you know. At this point, you are not committing—just exploring. The call comes from God, and nobody but you and he can know whether you have a priestly vocation.

There is plenty of time for your discernment to become clearer.

For Discernment of Religious Life

Lord,
I have heard your words, calling for men
to work in your vineyard.
I desire to serve you in a special way,
to devote my life to service of you and your Church.
But I don't feel that you are calling me to the
priesthood.
Do you wish me to forgo a wife and children
for a life focused on the kingdom?
Do you wish me to forgo a life of sanctification
through ordinary tasks
for a life of sanctity gained through careful
obedience to your will
through obedience to a rule and to a superior?
If you call, I will answer.
If you lead, I will follow.
If you do call me, give me the strength to say yes
and the peace to accept anything and everything
you have in mind for me.

For Discernment of Married Life

Lord,
I have opened my heart to the possibility

of serving you as a priest or member of a religious community.
I have asked you if this is what you want from me.
I am truly willing to say yes to this if this is what you will for me.
However, either in words or in silence,
you have made it clear that this is not my way.
Do you wish for me the awesome life of a husband and father?
Am I called to give myself freely to a woman— totally, faithfully and selflessly?
Am I called to be a natural father to children,
in the image of your Father?
I recognize the immense responsibility that comes with this vocation.
But I trust that you will walk with me
to guide, guard, and strengthen me and my future spouse.
Help me to find the woman to whom you have for all eternity desired me to be joined.

For Discernment of a Single Life

Lord,
I have opened my heart to the possibility of serving you
as a priest or member of a religious community.
I have asked you if this is what you want from me.

I am truly willing to say yes to this if this is what you will for me.
However, you have made it clear that this is not my way.
I have opened my heart to the possibility of loving a woman as I love myself
and to a life of sacrifice for her and my children.
I have asked you if this is what you want from me.
I am truly willing to say yes to this if this is what you will for me.
However, either in words or in silence, you have made it clear
that this is not my way right now.
Therefore, Lord, I am resolved to sanctify myself through a celibate life as a single man,
dedicating my work, my relationships, and my leisure to you.
Please use me in a way that will glorify you and bring others closer to you,
and let me know if you desire a new path for me in the future.

Remember that this is the one choice of life that is not necessarily permanent. God may be inviting you to remain single for the time being and call you to the priesthood, the religious life, or marriage later (even much later) in your life.

PRAYERS FOR WORK

FOR DISCERNMENT OF CAREER OR PARTICULAR EMPLOYMENT

It is important to be intentional when choosing a career or a particular employment opportunity. Spiritually, we acknowledge that from the moment of creation man was made for work (see Gen 2:15). Practically, we spend many of our waking hours engaged in our particular employment. Accordingly, we are wise to ask God to enter into our discernment. Obviously, we must recognize that God would not wish us to engage in work that presents an impediment to our moral life or a job that puts an undue burden on our family life. We should also be cognizant that any appropriate work done well can be a means to glorify God. It is also helpful to recognize that God wants us to be happy, so a job that we enjoy is a good thing.

Jesus,
much of your life was spent as a simple craftsman.
Day after day, you labored to earn a living

by the sweat of your brow.
You know what it is to work diligently and honestly.
You experienced the joy of learning your trade
from your foster father, Joseph,
and the blessings of working alongside him until his death.
I desire a job that is fulfilling—that I can do well
and that will pay me a just wage.
Help me to find a job or discern a career that will satisfy me
and bring me closer to you.

FOR EMPLOYMENT, IN DESPERATE NEED

Help me, O Lord,
as I am in desperate need of a job.
I know that you love me and are concerned for me.
I trust that you will somehow provide for me [and my family].
But right now, I am scared and I do not see a way forward.
I believe, but help my unbelief.
I trust, but help my lack of trust.
I give you my fears and my tears as my prayers.
Help me O Lord!

FOR DEDICATING ONE'S WORK TO GOD

In the book of Genesis, we learn that God created man to work. God intended man to work in harmony with him to cultivate and advance all creation. Because of the original sin of Adam and Eve, man's motivation for work is distorted and the created world does not fully cooperate with his efforts. Nevertheless, work remains a noble pursuit intended to be holy and to draw him closer to his Creator. Saint Josemaría Escrivá, like many other saints, reminds us that any work done well in a spirit of love is an act of heroic sanctification.

Lord Jesus,
you earned a living by the sweat of your brow for
many years.
You showed that the "work of your Father"
includes simple unacknowledged labor.
Every task was done for love of your Father.
Every task was done for love of your family.
Every task was done for love of us.
I offer up my work today as my prayer to you.
I offer up my work today as my prayer of love for
my family.
Every frustration and success,
every humiliation and compliment,

every moment of anguish or joy:
I give them all to you.

PRAYERS DURING THE WORKDAY

You probably encounter many pressures at work, especially if you work in a secular environment. Remember that God is stronger than any difficulties, temptations and wrongdoing you face in your workplace. "Trust in him, and he will act" (Ps 37:5).

For Honesty

"The end justifies the means" is often the unspoken motto of the workplace. Perhaps your co-workers are shirking their responsibilities but getting paid as much as or more than you. Perhaps you are tempted to help yourself to office supplies for your personal use, thinking that the company will not miss a box of pens or a ream of paper. You must endeavor to do well, even when you could get by with mediocrity. Jesus asks you to strive for perfection in all things, including honesty.

Lord, you humbled yourself and became a man like me.
You labored honestly.

You preached fearlessly.
You prayed incessantly.
You suffered intensely.
Give me the grace and strength to be honest, no matter the cost.
Help me humbly to accept where I am and what I have,
and not to covet that which I do not have (and do not need).
Your love and your grace—that's enough for me.

When You're Tired

Unfortunately, new technology does not make life much easier, but you are often told that you can and should be accomplishing more.

Being tired is an unfortunate reality and nothing to be embarrassed about. Be careful how you deal with it, though. Don't let it lead to irritability and lack of charity toward those around you. Nor do you want to slip into spiritual laziness, lowering your guard against temptation.

Like all things, tiredness can be an occasion for personal sanctification. With God's help, you can strengthen your resolve and move forward. Then, when appropriate, get the rest your mind and body require.

Father, I am tired,
but I will not give in or give up.
In my weakness may I rely on your strength.
I ask only for the grace to do what I need to do now.

IN FAILURE

It is a hard reality that even when you try your best, sometimes you fail. It may be that someone or something sabotaged your efforts, or it may be that your best efforts simply did not yield the anticipated result. Either way, you must accept the failure. Do not sulk, despair, or seek to deflect the blame. Give even your failure to God. He knows how hard it is for you to humble yourself, release the failure, and move on. Doing what you find hard is perhaps the greatest act of love you can offer him.

Father, you know how hard it is for me to accept this failure.
Everything in me wishes it would disappear.
While I do not understand in my head,
I know in my heart that my humble acceptance of this failure glorifies you.
Decrease my pride so that you may live within me.
I give this pain to you.

When Your Job Doesn't Satisfy You

You may not like your job: perhaps you are bored with it, or the work environment is unpleasant. There may be factors out of your control that prevent you from performing as you would like. Yet you must work to support yourself and possibly a family.

If after prayerful discernment, you decide that you cannot alter your work circumstances, you must endeavor to change your focus. Remember that you are working for God. Every day provides an opportunity to be a Christian witness at work—through your honesty, dedication, and charity to others. You can unite every hardship to the sufferings of Christ as a powerful prayer. And if you have a family, you can show your great love for your wife and children by carrying your cross for them every day.

Lord Jesus, you know my need to provide for
myself [and my family],
and you know my frustration in meeting that need.
If it is your will, change my situation.
In the meantime, grant me peace.
I trust that at this moment I am doing what you want
and that you will see me through this frustrating
time.

As always, I offer up everything to you, even my dissatisfaction.
Saint Joseph, humble and obedient father and worker, intercede for me.

For Accepting Authority

"Give back to Caesar what is Caesar's" (Mt 22:21, NIV). Our Lord made it clear that here on earth we will be subject to human authority, as he was subject to Mary and Joseph. Further, we may be subject to authority that is not loving or just. Jesus allowed the religious authorities to question him as if they were his superiors. The almighty God submitted himself to trial by his creatures and accepted their sentence of death.

Let go of your pride. Submit to the authority of those above you at work. Your humility and your peaceful example of love form an awesome prayer that can bring you and those around you to heaven.

Jesus, you loved me so much
that you became a slave and died for me.
Empty me of my pride.
Help me to accept the authority of those above me humbly.
Grant me the patience to accept wrongs done to me.

I need your help to listen,
not to complain, to smile,
to obey.
Make me more like you.

For Working with Subordinates

It is often difficult to be charitable toward subordinates. First, you must check your pride and not lord your authority over them. Next, you have to practice patience, mindful that they may not have the same level of intelligence, skills, experience, or motivation as you. Last, you must give your subordinates what you have been given. You must smile first. You must listen first. You must accept responsibility first. You must forgive first. Love comes before justice.

Father, as you teach, may I teach.
As you listen, may I listen.
As you forgive, may I forgive.
As you love, may I love.

It is perhaps even harder to be charitable toward a subordinate (or an equal) who is more gifted and motivated than you are! You might find such a person intimidating. You might fear that his or her superior abilities will embarrass you or even bring you a demotion.

This is a situation where your mettle will be tested, and you will have the opportunity to shine before God. Do not be jealous (coveting your neighbor's goods). Do not sabotage the person's efforts or put the person down ("killing" or bearing false witness). Rather, be a man—the best man you can be with what God has given you. Treat this person with respect and compassion. In other words, "Love your neighbor as yourself" (Lev 19:18).

Jesus, dispel my jealousy.
Quell my fear.
Help me humbly to accept myself as I am.
I want to be honest.
I want to be charitable.
But I can't be these without your help.

Against Gossip

Gossip is a big temptation in the workplace. There is unflattering talk about the boss, co-workers, clients, family, friends, politicians, sports stars, and celebrities. Gossip may be so prevalent in your life that you don't even realize you are participating in it.

Don't fool yourself by claiming that you have good motives or that you don't mean it badly. If no good is coming from your conversation, then your conversation is no good.

Endeavor to steer conversations away from gossip. If you can't do that, walk away. If you can't do that, at least be quiet.

Come, Holy Spirit.
Help me to love, not judge;
be silent, not gossip;
lead, not follow.

For Finding Balance

If you define yourself by your work, that's a pretty narrow definition. Your work did not create you. It does not love you. You can be replaced, and your work will not miss you. It will not visit you when you are old and infirm.

Must you work to support yourself and your family? Of course. But you must find balance in your life. Otherwise, you will be a son but have no parents. You will be married but have no wife. You will be a father but have no children. You will be Christian but have no God. You will die, and your work will die with you. Remember your everlasting definition: son of God! He wants you to "seek first his kingdom and his righteousness" (Mt 6:33).

Jesus, almighty Lord, Son, friend, teacher, and servant,
set my sights on you.
Be my example for work and prayer, love and leisure.
Steel me against the temptation to work for glory and riches.
Take my desire to provide and temper it with trust in your generosity.
Help me to work hard and then leave my work when appropriate.
Help me to be the [son, husband, father, friend] you wish me to be.

For Facing Retirement

Because of all the time you have spent engaged in your work, it has become a significant element in your life. Now that you are looking at retirement, you may feel as if you are leaving a part of you behind.

Your entire life has been a series of changes, some subtle and others more pronounced, but retirement seems like a drastic one. Look at it as one more step forward in your journey toward eternal happiness in heaven. It is not merely an end but another new beginning.

Father, I come before you humbly
and lay all of my life's work at your feet.
Forgive me for my shortcomings,
and accept my successes as reflections of your
greatness.
Holy Spirit, comfort me and lead me forward!

PRAYERS FOR YOUR FAMILY

All of us, married and single, belong to families. This is where most of us find our primary vocation. The Second Vatican Council pointed to the family as the "first and vital cell of society", which "appears as the domestic sanctuary of the Church by reason of the mutual affection of its members and the prayer that they offer to God in common" (*Apostolicam Actuositatem*, no. 11). Pray for and with your "vital cell" every day.

MARITAL PRAYERS

To Be a Better Husband

No student, athlete, or businessman realistically expects success without constantly striving to improve. Why would we expect different for our marriage? Our role as husband is our primary vocation. We have stood before God and vowed to love and cherish our wife. We must work, every day, to be a better husband. But we are weak and selfish, and we will fail. So let us make sure to pray for God's help regularly.

Lord,
you know that I love my wife
and that I want to be a good husband.
But I am weak
and seldom the man I wish to be.
So I need your grace and your strength,
not for my sake but for hers.
Help me to be a better husband.

Or simply:

Lord,
help me to be a better husband.

For Your Wife's Spiritual Well-Being

Primary to your vocation as a married man is helping your spouse reach heaven. You must constantly love her, support her, and pray for her.

What account will you give to God when you stand before his throne if your wife enjoyed a beautiful home, fashionable clothes, and an expensive car but was spiritually barren? I assure you that "I was a good provider" will fall on deaf ears.

First, you must lead by example: live a holy life; attend Mass regularly; pray constantly; treat your wife with love and respect; be a great father to your children. Second, pray for your wife. Perhaps the greatest habit is to offer up a decade of the Rosary for her every day (see the section on the Rosary in the Devotions and Miscellaneous Prayers chapter at the end of this book, page 131). You might also use the following prayer:

Holy Spirit,
true God and Spouse of the Virgin Mary,
sanctify my wife.
Breathe new life into her,
and enkindle in her heart a burning love for you.
Grant her wisdom to know your will and strength to persevere.
Fill her with the joy that comes from humble obedience and holy purity.
Transform her into the perfect daughter you desire her to be,
and grant her eternal life with you.

For Spousal Understanding

"A man shall leave his father and mother and be joined to his wife, and the two shall become one flesh" (Mk 10:7–8; see Gen 2:24). This "one flesh" is neither you nor your wife but an amalgamation of both. You must humble yourself: your wife's point of view and her way of doing things are as good as, if not better than, yours.

You are called to be "one" with your wife. Therefore, you must strive to understand her concerns, her aspirations, her identity—no matter how difficult that may be.

Jesus,
I do not fully understand my wife.
I don't know why she does not see things
as I do.
Yet I love her and want to love her even
more.
Help me swallow my pride and show her
the respect she deserves.
Grant me understanding.
If I cannot understand, grant me faith.
When I lack faith, give me trust.

In Times of Marital Crisis

Lord God,
my wife and I stood before you
and vowed to love and serve each other until
death.

You know what we are now going through.
You know how it has rocked the very foundation of our marriage.
Everything seems hopeless.
I do not see a way forward.
But you do.
If it is your will, show us that way.
If not, carry us as we collapse into your embrace.
Jesus, I trust in you!

For a Sick Spouse

It can be difficult to love your wife when she is ill or simply not feeling her best. You might fall into the habit of belittling her suffering; at other times you might make too much of it. While you cannot always say and do the right thing, you can always pray for your wife.

Lord, I place my wife and her affliction in your tender care.
Please console her and heal her.
Help her feel your presence in this dark time.
Holy Spirit,
fill me with wisdom;
guide my words and actions.

A Widower's Prayer

"'For this reason a man shall leave his father and mother and be joined to his wife, and the two shall become one flesh.' So they are no longer two but one flesh" (Mk 10:7–8). However, for you, the two have been torn apart. Your wife has left and you feel very much alone. How are you to go on, day after day? By remembering that nothing, not even death, can completely separate you. Your wife and you are still very much connected emotionally and spiritually, if not physically. Your wife is alive. She is with our Lord; she has entered into the fullness of eternity and is actually more connected to you than ever before. Talk to her. Pray for her. Pray to her (for her intercession).

Lord,
you created my wife for me
and me for her.
I love her.
I miss her.
Yet I trust that she is in your loving care.
And as you are always with me, so she will be
with me as well.
Grant my wife eternal joy with you.

And at my death reunite us,
together with all our loved ones.

PRAYERS FOR YOUR CHILDREN

For Your Children's Spiritual Well-Being

How important is it to you that your children have good grades in school, have many friends, and succeed in sports and other activities? How much time do you spend helping your children with their homework, driving them to band practice, or watching them play soccer? Now compare that with how much time you spend supporting your children in their spiritual journeys.

Your daughter's soccer statistics and your son's history grade are not indicative of their spiritual health. While these can be legitimate concerns, success in athletics and academics will not necessarily help them love their neighbor better or grow in their relationship with God. You must show your children the way to heaven—by your words and example. And you must pray for them.

Father, you have given me beautiful children.
I want them to love you here on earth

and live forever with you in heaven.
Fill them with your grace.
Send down your Spirit upon them.
Grant them faith, hope, and love.
Protect them from evil,
and show them the way to you.

For Patience with Children

While your children bring you pride and joy, they also cause you great consternation. Don't they understand that you are telling them the truth? Don't they understand that you know best?

First, you must change your attitude. You are not always right. And even when you are right, you must understand that your children are autonomous individuals, walking their own paths. You made mistakes, and they will make mistakes. They cannot always see things the way you do, because they are not you.

If you wish to teach your children, you must do so with love. Then you must pray and wait. Lack of patience will only lead to further misunderstanding and resistance. To grow in patience, you must grow in love and faith: love for your Lord and love for your children, faith in your Lord and faith in your children.

Lord Jesus, you know my great pain:
my children do not understand my direction,
and I have run out of patience.
This hurts because I love my children very much.
I cannot raise them well on my own.
I need your help.
These children are more yours than mine.
Help me trust that in your love for them, you will protect them.
I ask for the grace of patience.
Even if my children do not understand my opinion,
may they know that I love them.
Saint Joseph, father of my Lord,
intercede for me, that I may be a good father.

FOR A SICK CHILD

Jesus, I know you love my child.
I know you are intimately aware of [his, her] pain.
I know that even before I ask,
you know how much I want my child to be healed.
I give this child back to you.
I place [him, her] in your loving arms,
and I trust in your will for this child.
Jesus, I trust in you!

For a Child or Grandchild Who Has Left the Church

What can you do about your child who has left the Church? You must live a loving witness to the faith. You must encourage, but never nag. You must pray. You must forgive yourself for any perceived fault of your own that led to your child's departure. And you must not lose hope. God loves your child infinitely more than you do. God greatly desires this child of his to return home. God patiently awaits this child's return like the father of the prodigal son (Lk 15:11–32). Learn from this divine, patient trust. You know not the hour when or means by which this might be accomplished.

Father,
you know my angst over my child's departure
from your Church.
You know how I worry for [his, her] soul.
You know how much I desire that [he, she] would
return to the faith
that I sought to impart to [him, her].
I can do no more than pray.
So I ask you to touch my child's heart.
I trust that in your great love, you will answer
my prayer.

I know that you will never cease reaching out,
even to the last second of my child's life.
I give this child of mine into your care and
protection.
Jesus, I trust in you!

For a Child in an Unhealthy Relationship

Father,
I perceive that my child is in an unhealthy
relationship.
I fear that [he, she] is in serious danger.
I am powerless to help.
But I know that you love my child even more
than I do,
and for you, all things are possible.
So I entrust my child to your loving protection.
Speak to my child.
Convict my child of the truth.
Shield my child from danger.
Bring my child into your kingdom.

PRAYERS FOR SPECIAL FAMILY NEEDS

You are convinced that you are responsible for every aspect of your family's well-being: it is your absolute responsibility to feed, clothe, house, teach, and protect your children. You feel this way because you are a good husband and father. But in fact you are not entirely responsible for anything, because you are not the Creator. You cannot will your wife to come out of her depression. You cannot will your company not to downsize. You cannot will your child's broken leg to heal. God made the universe and everything in it, not you. God created your children, not you. God gave you every ability you have, and he alone sustains your every heartbeat (and those of your wife and your children). Do the best you can, and then let God be responsible for everything else.

IN TIMES OF FINANCIAL CRISIS

O Lord, my God, help me!
The world is closing in around me, and
I don't know what to do.
You made me and gave me everything
I have,
and yet it doesn't seem to be enough.
You are my God.
You are my Creator.
You are my provider.
Give me what I need; that is all I ask.
Jesus, I trust in you! Jesus, I trust in you!
Jesus, I trust in you!

For Healing of a Friend or Family Member

Jesus, Divine Physician,
you constantly reached out to the sick and suffering
during your time here on earth,
and you healed the multitudes.
I know that you love _____
and that you desire [his, her] good.
Look with mercy upon _____
and lay your healing hands upon [him, her].
I ask for [his, her] complete healing—mind,
body, soul, and spirit.
Jesus, I trust in you!

For Healing of Family Relationships

You would think that your relationships with your parents, siblings, and children would be your best. However, often just the opposite is true. These are the people with whom you interact most personally and emotionally. Therefore, these are the relationships that are the most fraught with potential conflict.

Forgiveness and acceptance are the keys to good family relationships. You must constantly forgive family members for what they have done and what they are doing, and you must work at accepting them, rather than trying to change them.

To love someone does not mean you have to like everything about the person. Love is first a choice, then a commitment.

Lord God,
I did not choose my family.
Rather, you have placed these people in my life.
I believe you have done so for a reason,
even though I don't understand that reason.
As hard as it is sometimes,
I forgive them for what they have done;
I accept them for who they are;
and I love them.
Jesus, teach me how to love as you love.
Holy Spirit, guide my thoughts, words, and actions;
grant us peace and freedom from conflict.
Saint Joseph, spouse of the Blessed Virgin,
foster father of my Lord, and son of God:
intercede for me.

PRAYERS FOR PARENTS AS THEY AGE

Your relationship with your aging mother and father can be very challenging. Their need for your support is increasing, while you are busy with your own life. Adding to the challenge is the fact that your parents are becoming slower in their movements, tend to repeat themselves, don't understand what you're saying, and are perhaps rather cantankerous. Sometimes you find it hard to talk to them on the phone without having your blood pressure rise.

Even if they were not your parents, you would be obliged to afford them the respect they deserve as a beloved son and daughter of God. And because they are your parents, you must double your efforts to treat them with love, patience, and respect. The fourth commandment is clear: "Honor your father and your mother" (Ex 20:12, Deut 5:16).

For Aging Parents

Loving Father,
pour out your tender mercy upon my parents.
Strengthen them in their infirmity;
comfort them in their loneliness;
assure them of their great dignity in your eyes;
inspire them to love and desire you more;
and grant them peace.

For Strength in Caring for Aging Parents

You are called to love, honor, and care for your aging parent to the best of your ability. But this can be very challenging. It is tough seeing a parent degrade physically, mentally, and emotionally. Further, there is no assurance that your parent will age gracefully or accept help graciously. Rather, caring for an aging parent will likely push your patience to the very limit. Pray for strength, do the best you can, and forgive yourself for your many perceived failures.

Father,
help me not only to love my parents in my heart,
but also to act in that love.
Grant me strength to listen to them attentively,
respect their opinions,
affirm their dignity,
and patiently bear whatever annoys me.
I offer my frustrations as a prayer
for their spiritual and physical well-being.

PRAYERS FOR PERSONAL STRENGTH

No matter what life seems to throw at you, God is in charge. Even your personal weaknesses and "favorite sins" are opportunities for him to work. "Rejoice always, pray constantly, give thanks in all circumstances; for this is the will of God in Christ Jesus for you" (1 Thess 5:16–18).

IN SICKNESS

Because you are sick, it is likely that you are tired and unhappy. It would be easy to make those around you miserable as well. Don't.

You have to make efforts to be pleasant when you are sick. Accept your discomfort and offer it as a prayer for those you love. Or if you really want to be heroic, offer it up for people who bother you. Don't be a martyr, though. See a doctor. Admit to those around you that you are sick, and let them help you. Sometimes letting someone do something for you is the greatest kindness you can show that person.

Lord Jesus,
Help me embrace this "little cross" of sickness today.
I unite my discomfort with your great Passion as a prayer for others.
Grant me patience and charity above my strength.

IN SERIOUS OR CHRONIC ILLNESS

Your physical suffering is hard enough to bear, but you also face feelings of fear, anger, despair, helplessness, and worthlessness. There is only one way to endure this misery, only one way to give this suffering any meaning: you must transform your suffering into prayer.

The greatest saints are of accord on this point: pain and suffering lovingly endured and offered for others is exceedingly powerful prayer! You have the opportunity to unite your pain to the Passion of our Lord Jesus Christ for the salvation of souls. What greater gift can you possibly give to God than accepting what is burdensome and loving what is repugnant? As Christ carried his cross for all of us, carry yours for those you love.

Lord Jesus,
walk with me on this road of pain and sorrow.
Help me embrace the cross that is upon me.
Give me the strength to carry it.
Assist me when my strength is spent.
Teach me to die to myself in order to live for others.
Accept my pain and anguish as prayer.
I offer it all to you for [your prayer intention].

IN TIMES OF GREAT DOUBT AND DESPAIR

O Lord! My Lord! My God!
Hear my cries.
See my tears.
Know my pain.
I am in a pit.
I do not see the light.
And I have no hope.
Hear me, because you promised you would!
Help me, because you promised you would!
Heal me, because you promised you would!
O Lord! My Lord! My God!

WHEN STRUGGLING WITH MENTAL ILLNESS

Struggling with mental illness can be one of the hardest crosses to bear. There is no outward wound. There is often a lack of understanding in those around you. It can affect you mentally, physically, emotionally, and spiritually. You feel alone. You lose hope.

Mental illness is as real as any other illness. It is not your fault that you suffer from it. God loves you in the depth of your suffering. He does not desire you to suffer, but for the time being allows it. Pray for our Lord to take the cross away. If he will not at this point, ask him to walk with you and help you carry this cross of suffering. Seek to accept the suffering for the time being and ask that through this acceptance, this suffering might be a prayer to help someone else.

Cry when you need to cry. Tell Jesus that you love him. Ask him to help you feel his love for you. Also, do not be ashamed of mental illness. Share your suffering with those who love you, and seek professional help.

God my Father,
you know my pain and anguish,

my anxiety and my fear.
Sometimes, I feel that I cannot bear the weight of this affliction.
Everything seems dark.
Hope is hard.
Yet I know you love me,
and I recognize that you sacrificed your Son for me.
Take this cross from me if it is your will.
If not, help me to bear this burden.
When I cannot, ask your Son to carry it for me.
Help me trust you.
Help me hope.
Help me just get through this day.

FOR FACING THE PROCESS OF AGING (AND DEATH)

You are going to die. This is a hard reality, but it must be faced courageously.

The certainty of death requires us to examine why we live, how we live, and what follows death. Jesus assured us that death is not the end and modeled this truth for us. Rather, we are destined for eternal peace and joy with God. Jesus' followers were so fully convinced of this truth that they went cheerfully to their martyrdom rather than deny it.

We must ponder death from time to time—not out of morbid curiosity, but with the goal of gaining hope from its certitude.

The hope of the resurrection gives meaning to life. We are not mere happenstance. Our lives have purpose. We are each intentionally created by a God who loves us and desires us to receive his love for all eternity. He loved us so much that he suffered, died, and rose from the dead in order to open the gates of heaven for us. The hope of the resurrection is the remedy for all suffering and fear—all pain and fear in this life will ultimately give way to unfathomable joy.

As we age, the fear of death is not necessarily our primary concern. Rather, many of us find it most difficult to accept the reality of physical degradation and the fear of increased pain and suffering. The (difficult) remedy for this is to (1) focus on the good—praising God and thanking him for all of the blessings in our life, (2) accept that pain that is unavoidable and, by giving willful assent to it, offer the pain up as prayer for others, and (3) constantly make acts of hope (see the Act of Hope in the chapter Prayers for Any Time, page 32).

God my Father,
I am slowing down.

I have many pains.
And one day I will die.
Yet, I trust that you made me not for death, but
for life!
You made me not for pain, but for joy!
You made me not for fear, but for love!
Thank you for my life.
Thank you for all of those whom I love.
Thank you for the wonders of creation.
Thank you for becoming man, suffering, and
dying for me.
I accept my suffering.
And in so accepting it, I give it to you
as a prayer for [state your intention].
I hope in your promise that one day
I am to be with you in paradise.

FOR PATIENCE WITH A PERSON WHO ANNOYS YOU

Sure, you desire to "love your neighbor as yourself" (Mk 12:31), yet there are people who bother you greatly. Maybe it is the way they talk, their mannerisms, or everything about them. Sometimes even being in the same room with them can be unbearable.

Take comfort in knowing that some of the most loving saints experienced the same thing. You cannot change the person who annoys you. You can, however, acknowledge two things in your heart: (1) God created this person purposefully, and (2) God loves this person personally. Remember that your slightest act of kindness toward him or her is an act of love for God.

Lord,
help me love this person, because you do.
To the extent that I cannot love,
help me tolerate this person out of love
for you.

Or pray simply:

Lord, for you!

PRAYERS FOR FIGHTING ADDICTIONS

Even if you are not a drug addict or an alcoholic, you may be seeking solace in something other than God. Do you use cigarettes, alcohol, medications, or food to relax, "take the edge off", or put yourself in a better mood?

That is not to say that every use of any of these substances is a sin. But you must honestly face these questions: How much? How often? Why? What is the effect on me and those whom I love?

In miraculously turning water into wine and multiplying the fish and loaves of bread, our Lord was certainly not condoning drunkenness and gluttony. Rather, he was teaching us that he will provide for our true needs.

In Serious Addiction

Do not be ashamed to admit to a serious addiction; every man has weaknesses. The strong man admits his and seeks to overcome them.

Failing to acknowledge your addiction and seek help will only harm you and torture those who love you. There is no weakness for which God cannot provide strength. In fact, God told Saint Paul, "My power is made perfect in weakness" (2 Cor 12:9). Admit your addiction, get help, and pray!

O God, my Father, help me! I am so weak!
I cannot beat this addiction without your help and the help of others.
I surrender myself to you
and to the care of those who can help me.

While I cannot take proper care even of myself,
I trust that you will take care of everyone and
everything I love.
I know that you understand me,
that you forgive me,
and that you love me.
And because of this I will not lose hope.

For Appropriate Use of Alcohol

Just because you do not drink every day or drive drunk does not mean that you are not abusing alcohol. Do you think you need alcohol to relax, have fun, and be sociable? A couple of drinks with dinner or with friends can be extremely enjoyable, but are you a social user or a social abuser?

Consider the effect alcohol is having on you. How is it affecting your health, productivity, and relationships with others? If you are a husband and father, honestly look at how your alcohol use affects your marriage and what example you are setting for your children. Look to God and not to a drink for help. Pray for the strength to be the man he calls you to be. (Note: The prayer below is not for the alcoholic but for those who occasionally abuse alcohol. The alcoholic needs to abstain totally.)

Lord, I humbly admit that I sometimes abuse
alcohol.
You know that I do not wish to hurt myself, my
family, or anyone else.
You know that I am well-intentioned but weak.
Give me the awareness of the right time and right
amount.
Give me the courage to avoid situations of temptation.
Give me the strength to control my intake.
Keep me ever mindful of my love for and
responsibility toward my family and friends.

Against Addiction to Nicotine

Is it manly to use nicotine? Is it healthy? Does it make you more pleasant or attractive? Do you want others (especially children) in your life to follow your example?

You must examine very carefully (and very honestly) how you use nicotine, why you use it, how much you use it, and how your use affects others.

Lord,
help me truly understand
That my body is "a temple of the Holy Spirit"
(1 Cor 6:19).
Give me the desire and strength

to treat my body, which you created in your
image, appropriately.
Help me not turn to bad habits and drugs
as false crutches for my emotional and physical
challenges.
Strengthen me for my own good
and for the good of those around me.

For Moderation in Eating

Why do you order the sixteen-ounce T-bone when the eight-ounce filet is more than enough? Why do you order the fries when the sandwich is huge, or the dessert when you have already had four courses?

In the Catholic Church, celebration calls for feasting. Yet not every meal is meant to be a feast. You want to be happy, but does that mean being full? The happiness that you desire far surpasses that which food can provide. And it is spiritual fullness, not a full stomach, that you really seek.

God created a beautiful world with many sensory delights that he wants you to enjoy. But every created thing is beautiful only because it reflects God's infinite beauty, and only dimly. God—who gives himself to us as food in the Eucharist—is the perfect, all-satisfying entrée, and everything else in the world is merely the bread served before dinner.

The rolls will never satisfy you, and if you eat too many, you will lose your appetite for the entrée.

Remember, some amount of hunger can be good. Let it remind you to be hungry for God and for heaven.

A true man is not a slave to his appetites but struggles always to master them. If you are resisting temptation, offer up your hunger as a prayer for those whom you love.

Father,
help me enjoy your gifts in moderation.
And help me trust that you will always provide
for my needs.
Let me never be satisfied by the things of this
world,
and keep me hungry for you.

When you're tempted to overindulge:

Lord, this won't satisfy me. Only you!

DURING A FAITH CRISIS

Do you question your faith? Do you doubt God's existence sometimes? You are not alone. Every man has doubts. Sometimes they are fleeting; other times they last for prolonged periods of time.

In times of doubt, remember that faith is a gift from God, not your own accomplishment. You do not merit faith or reason your way to it; you receive faith. Faith is not about feelings. It is about saying yes to God, even (and especially) when it is difficult to do so.

The greatest prayer for faith and in faith is that of the father of the possessed boy in Mark 9:24. Cry out as he did when your faith is weak:

Lord, I do believe; help my unbelief!

PRAYERS FOR PURITY

It is important to understand that *all* men, no matter their state in life (married, single, or priest/religious), are called to be chaste. That is, they are all called to temperance (or complete abstinence) in the indulgence of the sexual appetite. Most priests and religious (there are some exceptions in the Eastern Church) are called to complete abstinence from the sexual act. Single men are also called to this complete abstinence (despite the strong voice against this in our secular culture). A married man is called to abstain from sexual relations with any woman except his spouse.

The sexual act is not meant to be a quick "high", but perhaps the most intimate complete gift of oneself to another—of one man to one woman and one woman to one man. The sexual act is also called the "marital act", as it is ordered to marriage—to the dual (inseparable) goals of spousal unity and procreation.

Sexual addictions and addiction to pornography have reached pandemic levels. If you are engaging in sexual encounters (not with your wife), you are putting your (and another person's) mind, body, and soul at serious risk. If you are viewing pornography (and likely masturbating), you are reshaping your brain, dulling your ability to enjoy the beauty of the marital act, contributing to the depersonalizing of the actors of that pornography, and putting your soul in peril. Unchecked, these addictions will lead to an inability to engage in a healthy relationship with the opposite sex or a spouse. They will leave you depressed, unfulfilled, and incapable of the level of joy our Lord wishes for you.

That having been said, God does not hate you because of this addiction. You are still absolutely beautiful and beloved to him! God does not want you to wallow in shame or give in to despair. He wants you to be free of this burden. He wants you to be happy, healthy, and holy! If you are called to marriage, God wants you to experience the true joy that results from a properly oriented, loving relationship with a spouse.

There is hope. You *can* heal. You can find a joy that will far surpass these quick sexual highs you have experienced. To heal, you will need to pray, but you must also seek help. There are many great avenues for treatment of these addictions. Look for a good (preferably Christian/Catholic) program or health care professional. Do it now!

Lord,
I've lost control.
I can't see the beauty that is marital love
and am attracted to a distorted shadow of this true love.
I don't want to be, but I am.
Help me, Lord!
Help me see the beauty of man and woman as you created them.
Help me recognize others and myself as your beloved children,
not mere objects to be used for pleasure.
Help me!
Heal me!

PRAYERS FOR PURITY

If you are honest with yourself, you will admit that sexual purity is difficult (even if you are not addicted to pornography). Temptations are everywhere.

A married man might say to himself, "I have never given in; I have never cheated on my wife." An unmarried man might say, "I'm not sleeping with anyone." These are, however, merely the first steps to holy purity.

How many pornographic images do you see on the internet? How many crude texts do you receive from friends? How long do your eyes rest on the attractive woman walking in front of you? What kind of movies do you watch? What is it in those ads on your social media/news feeds that attracts your attention? Are your actions throughout the day focused on growing in the love and respect you have for your wife, girlfriend or women in general? Or, do you constantly seek little sexual excitements?

Men are under attack, and you may not win every battle. But you must always keep up the fight. Your body, the body of your wife or girlfriend and the bodies of all men and women are temples of the Holy Spirit and must be treated as such. Your sexuality is an awesome gift from God to be enjoyed, but it is to be enjoyed lovingly and appropriately.

For Marital Purity

Blessed Mother,
you are the most beautiful woman of all creation.
Help me appreciate your beauty, reflected in my wife:

the beauty of God's love.
Intercede for me to your Son, Jesus,
that I may receive the strength to avoid impurity.

For Purity in Dating

Blessed Mother,
you remained pure and faithful out of love for our Lord.
Help me appreciate your beauty, reflected in all women:
the beauty of God's love.
Intercede for me to your Son, Jesus,
that I may receive the strength to avoid impurity
and that I might prepare myself for the woman whom I will one day wed.

For Defense of the Senses

Pornography is everywhere: the internet transmits pornography and sexual enticements; sexual acts are depicted in every form of mainstream media; pictures of women in their undergarments (or less) are plastered on billboards and buses and show up as ads on your news and social media feeds. How can you avoid seeing these things? The answer is, you cannot, but you can avoid staring. Don't give in to the temptation to look "just a bit longer".

And get help. There are many great resources out there!

Lord, I am weak and need your help, right now!
Turn my heart to you.

Or:

Give me strength to be pure, O Lord!

Or:

I want to be pure for you, Mary!

DEDICATION OF THE BODY

Your body is a "temple of the Holy Spirit" (1 Cor 6:19). Are you going to profane the temple of God by using it for illicit sexual purposes? Or will you answer Saint Paul's call to "glorify God in your body" (1 Cor 6:20)? Your body is awesome! Your sexuality is a gift from God. But use the gift properly. Praise God in the temple of your body.

Father, you have created me in your image and likeness.

You have given me a body
and sent your Spirit to dwell within it.
I offer up my entire body to you.
May my eyes look at you.
May my ears listen to your Word.
May my mouth praise you.
May my legs carry me to you.
May my arms do your work.
My sexuality is a gift from you to me [and to my wife or future wife].
May I praise you by using this gift lovingly and purely.

PRAYERS IN DEATH

The death of a loved one is heart-wrenching. You have lost the company of someone whose life enriched yours, someone whose presence made your life fuller and happier. And you have come face-to-face with mortality.

Let the death of your loved one remind you of your deepest belief: God made you to be perfectly happy with him—not just for ten, forty, or ninety years, but for eternity.

FOR ONE WHO HAS DIED

Do not try to figure out why your loved one died. Thank God for the gift of this person in your life. Pray for this person's soul. And pray for the consolation of all who grieve over this loss.

Father,
in your image you created _____;
with your love you endowed [him, her];
in your generosity, you shared [him, her];

in your compassion, you redeemed [him, her];
in your wisdom, you recalled [him, her].
In your mercy, forever cleanse [him, her];
in your house, forever keep [him, her];
and in your heart, forever love [him, her].

Here is a traditional prayer for one who has died and for the souls in purgatory:

Eternal rest grant unto [him, her], O Lord,
and let perpetual light shine upon [him, her].
May [his, her] soul and the souls of all the faithful
departed,
through the mercy of God, rest in peace.
Amen.

PRAYERS FOR A PARENT WHO HAS DIED

Although your mother or father has died, the time for conversation with your parents is not over. Thank your parent for cooperating with God to give you life and for the love and support given to you. Forgive your parent for any hurt he or she may have caused you. Let your parent's good works live through your life, and let his or her mistakes be buried forever. Pray for your parent's triumphant reception into heaven and for your eventual reunion there with all whom you love.

After the Death of a Father

O God,
into your loving care I commend my father.
His weary journey is over,
and he is ready to come home.
Call to him—you, his Father and Lord;
call him to yourself.
Release his burdens,
and lift him up into heaven.
Grant my father eternal joy,
and reunite us one day in your kingdom.

After the Death of a Mother

Lord Jesus,
you who are the Son of the Blessed Mother,
I plead to you on behalf of my own mother.
When I was infirm, she carried me;
now lift her up on eagles' wings.
When I was hungry, she fed me;
now nourish her with the bread of angels.
When I was sad, she comforted me;
now fill her with perfect happiness.
When it was time, she brought me into this life;
now grant her eternal life with you.

Always she loved me;
now, and forever more, envelop her in your infinite love.

AFTER THE DEATH OF A SPOUSE

"The two shall become one" (Mt 19:5). And now you have seemingly been ripped apart, for your wife does not walk with you in life anymore. Yet everything she is permeates everything you are. You carry her with you everywhere you go, in this life and into eternity. Pray for your wife. Pray with her. Thank her, forgive her, love her, and trust that our Lord has called her home for a reason.

Good Saint Joseph,
my patron and constant help,
my wife has gone where I cannot yet follow.
So I ask you to walk with her instead.
Present my beautiful bride to our Lord,
and speak tenderly on her behalf.
O Mary,
Queen of Heaven and mother of all,
lead your daughter up to the throne,
and place her in the embrace of her merciful Savior.
Mary and Joseph,

intercede for my wife and for me,
that we may be united with our Lord forever.

AFTER THE DEATH OF A CHILD

Everything about this death seems to be madness. You should have watched your child grow and mature. Your child should have buried you one day. Your child should not have died. Yet in the utter depths of pain and despair, you are offered hope.

Place your trust in God and his promises. He created you and your child in immeasurable love. He does not confine his love to the few brief moments we spend here on earth. God knew you and your child and loved both of you before he even created you, and he will love both of you together for all eternity.

Our Lord weeps with you right now, as he wept at the death of Lazarus. But God's love for your child is unfathomable, and his design for your child is eternal joy. This is your sure hope.

Come, O heavenly host of angels,
and joyfully bear my child home to heaven.
Rejoice, you saints and martyrs,
and welcome [his, her] triumphant arrival.

O Mary, Queen of Heaven,
take my [son, daughter] gently by the hand,
and present [him, her] before the throne of your Son.
O sweet Jesus,
receive back your most precious gift to me,
and grant that one day I may join [him, her] forever in your loving embrace.

IN THE DEPTHS OF DESPAIR

Can you understand why your loved one died? No, not now; maybe never. But can you hope? Yes, and you must! "Hope does not disappoint us, because God's love has been poured into our hearts through the Holy Spirit who has been given to us" (Rom 5:5).

When the depths of despair threaten you, pray:

Hear my prayer, O Lord;
let my cry come to you!
In my loss I am lost.
I do not know what to do.
Carry me, for I cannot walk.
Feed me, for I am starving.
I have nothing but my grief.

Bear it for me, Lord.
Sustain me for just this moment;
I cannot even imagine the next.

You can only see the "now", which is your grief. Pray this prayer for now. Look for God's comfort now. Tomorrow will come, and God will continue to be with you.

THE MASS

What is the Mass? Entire books have been devoted to answering this question, and it is important for you to endeavor, throughout your life, continually to come to a better understanding of and love for the Mass. That having been said, it is important to have a simple understanding of the Mass as well—one that you can hold on to in your heart and that you can share with others easily.

The Mass is an opportunity for us to encounter Jesus in the most perfect and personal way here on earth.

The Mass is the re-presentation of our Lord's sacrifice of his life for our salvation. As our Lord's act of suffering, death, and resurrection is an eternal act that pervades all time, we are invited to enter into this act spiritually and to receive the fruits of this salvific act in every Mass.

The Mass is an opportunity to receive the Body, Blood, Soul, and Divinity of our Lord. Holy Communion means just that—we are enabled to come into communion with the Real Presence of God.

The Mass is the central act of worship in the life of a Catholic. Yes, we can pray to God anywhere at any time, but no private prayer compares to the efficacy of Mass. At the Mass, we worship the Lord of creation via the specific means Christ instituted for us at the Last Supper, directing us to continually "do this in memory of [him]".

DO I NEED TO ATTEND MASS?

Yes, you do, on every Sunday and every holy day of obligation (for example, Christmas, Easter, and the Immaculate Conception). But you can actually attend every day if you feel so called.

The Church teaches as an unwavering moral rule that we are to "honor the Sabbath" by attending Mass every Sunday. We are also called to attend Mass on several holy days of obligation, which are defined by the Church but can vary from diocese to diocese. You can find ample explanation for this online, so let us, for purposes of this simple guide, just reflect on a few reasons.

God loves you! He is waiting to give himself to you—Body, Blood, Soul, and Divinity—and to speak to you through scripture, prayers, and the homily. He instituted the Mass as a moment of loving encounter and spiritual fulfillment for you personally.

We need to worship God and thank him for everything he is and does. The Mass is the perfect vehicle for this, which our Lord himself established and asks us to participate in.

We succeed at nothing in life to which we fail to apply discipline. There is no hope of excelling in sports, work, or any relationship without the discipline of effort and constancy. Why would we ever believe that we need to show up at work every day, but we can just worship God whenever we feel like doing so?

PREPARATION FOR MASS

Men aim to arrive well before their golf tee time in order to have ample time to stretch, hit some balls, and practice putting. On Sunday mornings, we often come peeling into the church parking lot minutes before Mass and hustle our family into the last pew, hoping to time our arrival at the pew ten seconds before the priest begins processing down the aisle. This is unfortunate. Let's work to change this habit.

It is an excellent habit to arrive in our pew at least five to ten minutes before Mass starts. We should kneel (at least for a period of time and then maybe sit quietly) and direct our attention to the altar and tabernacle. We should acknowledge God's presence in the tabernacle and remind ourselves that soon, our Lord will be made present in the bread and wine offered upon the altar. We should quiet our minds and dispel any distractions.

Prayers Before Mass

My Lord and my God,
I firmly believe that you are here—truly present in the tabernacle;
I know that you see me;
that you hear me.
I know that you will be made present in the bread and wine
offered on the altar,
And that you invite me to receive you,
Body, Blood, Soul, and Divinity, at Communion.
I put away all concerns and cares,
and desire to live this next hour focused solely on you.

Or:

My Lord and my God.
I know that you are here.
Help me focus only on you for the next hour.

Or:

Almighty and ever-living God,
I approach the sacrament of your only-begotten Son,
our Lord Jesus Christ.
I come sick to the doctor of life,
unclean to the fountain of mercy,
blind to the radiance of eternal light,
poor and needy to the Lord of heaven and earth.
Lord, in your great generosity,
heal my sickness, wash away my defilement,
enlighten my blindness, enrich my poverty,
and clothe my nakedness.
May I receive the bread of angels,
the King of kings and Lord of lords,
with humble reverence,
with the purity and faith,
the repentance and love
and the determined purpose
that will help to bring me to salvation.
May I receive the sacrament of the Lord's
Body and Blood
and its reality and power.
Kind God,
may I receive the Body of your only-begotten Son,
our Lord Jesus Christ,
born from the womb of the Virgin Mary,

and so be received into his mystical Body
and numbered among his members.
Loving Father,
as on my earthly pilgrimage
I now receive your beloved Son
under the veil of a sacrament,
may I one day see him face-to-face in glory,
who lives and reigns with you forever.
Amen.

ATTRIBUTED TO SAINT THOMAS AQUINAS

SHOULD I RECEIVE THE EUCHARIST?

The Church encourages us to receive Communion devoutly and frequently. However, there are circumstances under which we should not receive. First of all, to receive, we must be baptized Catholic. We must approach the Eucharist with at least a basic level of belief or firm desire to believe that this is the Body, Blood, Soul, and Divinity of Jesus, although it is all right to have doubts. Also, we must not be conscious of any grave unconfessed sin. If there is a serious sin on our heart, we should plan to go to confession (see the chapter on the Sacrament of Reconciliation). Normally, we should have fasted for one hour prior to receiving Holy

Communion. If you have any questions whether these conditions apply to you, ask your parish priest.

There are situations where a current life condition prevents us from receiving Communion (for example, we have been divorced and have remarried without receiving an annulment of the first marriage). If this is your situation, please do not give up. Talk to your parish priest about your situation. The remedy may be easier than you think.

If it seems harsh or unfair that individuals should be told to abstain from receiving the Eucharist, it is important to better understand why. The Church does so out of love, not judgment. It seeks to foster the love and respect that the Eucharist deserves. This is not mere bread or wine, but the very substance of almighty God! And Saint Paul admonishes us that "whoever ... eats the bread or drinks the cup of the Lord in an unworthy manner will be guilty of profaning the body and blood of the Lord. Let a man examine himself, and so eat of the bread and drink of the cup. For any one who eats and drinks without discerning the body eats and drinks judgment upon himself" (1 Cor 11:27–29).

Do you desire to receive our Lord in the Eucharist? Awesome! Are you concerned that you might not be free to do so? That is all right. Do something about it. Talk to a priest. And, in the meantime, when at Mass, make a spiritual communion using the prayer below.

PRAYER OF SPIRITUAL COMMUNION

My Jesus, I believe that Thou art truly present in the Most Blessed Sacrament.
I love Thee above all things,
and I desire to possess Thee within my soul.
Since I am unable now to receive Thee sacramentally,
come at least spiritually into my heart.
I embrace Thee as being already there,
and unite myself wholly to Thee;
never permit me to be separated from Thee.

SAINT ALPHONSUS LIGUORI

Or:

I wish, my Lord, to receive you
with the purity, humility, and devotion
with which your most holy mother received you,
with the spirit and fervor of the saints.

TAUGHT TO SAINT JOSEMARÍA ESCRIVÁ AS A CHILD BY A PRIEST

There is a temptation to start running for the car after the priest says, "The Mass has ended. Let us now go in peace." There is no sin in doing so, but we would benefit from lingering a while. It is a great practice to just sit (or kneel) for a few moments and acknowledge the reality that God is truly present in us in a special way. This is a good time for thanking God for the Mass and the ability to receive him in Communion. It is also a time to ask God for grace to go forth and share the Good News of salvation with others (both by the example of our life and through words if the opportunity arises). Silent contemplation is fine. There are also some traditional prayers.

Anima Christi

Soul of Christ, sanctify me;
Body of Christ, save me;
Blood of Christ, inebriate me;
water from the side of Christ, wash me;
Passion of Christ, strengthen me;
O good Jesus, hear me;
within your wounds hide me;
separated from you, let me never be;
from the evil one protect me;

at the hour of my death, call me;
and close to you bid me; that with your saints,
I may be praising you forever and ever.

I Thank You, Lord

I thank You, Lord, Almighty Father, Everlasting God,
for having been pleased, through no merit of mine,
but of Your great mercy alone,
to feed me, a sinner, and Your unworthy servant,
with the precious Body and Blood of Your Son, our Lord Jesus Christ.
I pray that this Holy Communion
may not be for my judgment and condemnation,
but for my pardon and salvation.
Let this Holy Communion be to me an armor of faith
and a shield of good will,
a cleansing of all vices
and a rooting out of all evil desires.
May it increase love and patience,
humility and obedience, and all virtues.
May it be a firm defense against the evil designs
of all my visible and invisible enemies,
a perfect quieting of all the desires of soul and body.
May this Holy Communion bring about

a perfect union with You, the one true God,
and at last enable me to reach eternal bliss when
You will call me.
I pray that You bring me, a sinner,
to the indescribable Feast
where You, with Your Son and the Holy Spirit,
are to Your saints
true light, full blessedness, everlasting joy, and
perfect happiness.
Through the same Christ our Lord. Amen.

SAINT THOMAS AQUINAS

O Jesus, Meek and Humble of Heart

Simply say the following three times slowly:

O Jesus, meek and humble of heart,
Make my heart like unto thine.

WHEN MASS IS SPIRITUALLY DRY

Mass, like any other routine practice, can become dry. We can feel like we aren't getting anything out of it. We can be tempted to stop going. This is normal. We should feel no shame in this. But we must persevere.

We can't stop being a husband or father, or stop showing up for work because we "don't feel like it". Nor should we stop worshiping God or being fed at his table because "we don't feel like it". When things get dry, we must be mindful that faith is not a feeling, but a decision. Just as we vow to be faithful to a wife in the bad times as well as the good, we pledge our faith in God, both when we feel his presence and when we aren't even sure he exists.

Even if we feel no emotional high from the readings, homily, or reception of the Eucharist, all of these things are feeding us and building up grace within us. Perhaps we need to listen more carefully. Perhaps we need to prepare our hearts better by reception of the Sacrament of Confession. Maybe we do need to learn or meditate more upon the reality of what is happening at Mass. And maybe we just need to get through a dry spell and offer up that dryness and our constancy as a prayer of love to God, even if we don't feel his love at the moment.

THE SACRAMENT OF RECONCILIATION

WHAT IS CONFESSION?

The formal name for confession is the Sacrament of Reconciliation. These two names highlight a two-fold reality of the sacrament. First, we confess and take ownership of the fact that we have sinned; we have freely chosen to do that which is inapposite to love of God, love of our neighbor, and love of ourselves. And through this confession, we acknowledge that we have, to a lesser or greater extent depending on the gravity of our sin, distanced ourselves from a relationship with God. Second, because of this humble and honest confession, God forgives our sins completely and reconciles us to himself.

The Sacrament of Reconciliation is a great gift from God. Through his incarnation, suffering, death, and resurrection, Jesus took upon himself all of the sins of the world. He paid the price for all offenses against God. Jesus took upon himself the punishment that justice demanded. Through the Sacrament of Reconciliation, Jesus offers the infinite mercy of

God. Through this sacrament, we avail ourselves of the meritorious work of Jesus. Through this sacrament, we are completely forgiven of our sins and restored in our relationship with God.

WHY DO I NEED TO GO TO CONFESSION?

We all recognize that we are not perfect. We freely choose to sin. We act in a manner that is contrary to love for God, our neighbor, and ourself. It is not enough merely to recognize this truth in some general way. Jesus' first message of his public ministry was a call to repentance (see Mt 4:17, Mk 1:15). We are to acknowledge our sins, voice contrition for having committed them, and endeavor to turn away from these sins.

But why must we confess our sins to a priest? The quick answer is that Jesus told us to and gave his first priests—Peter and the other apostles—the power to forgive sins: "If you forgive the sins of any, they are forgiven; if you retain the sins of any, they are retained" (Jn 20:23). But it is helpful to remember that we are not really confessing our sins to a priest, but to Jesus. As a mere man, no priest can forgive sin and remove all punishment that would be due from that sin. However, in the

Sacrament of Reconciliation, the priest stands "in the person of Christ". Therefore, it is to Christ we are confessing our sins, and it is Christ who is forgiving our sins.

Theoretically, we could make a perfect act of contrition to God without involving a priest. But how likely is it that we have ever been or will ever be *perfectly* contrite—perfectly sorry for our sins with a perfect intention never to sin again? Fortunately, we don't have to worry about this, as our honest sorrow, even if imperfect, is enough through the Sacrament of Reconciliation.

How often should I go to confession? The simple answer is that you should go whenever you feel you must (without being overly scrupulous). Practically speaking, it is a good habit to go monthly.

PREPARATION FOR THE SACRAMENT OF RECONCILIATION

Prior to going to confession, it is important to undertake an examination of conscience. This is where we carefully and prayerfully review how we have lived our lives since we last availed ourselves of the Sacrament of Reconciliation. It is imperative that we identify all of our mortal sins. We should also identify our venial (less serious) sins to the extent we are practically able, especially those that are most frequent and those that most significantly hurt our relationship with God and do injury to others. There are many formal examinations of conscience available in churches and on Catholic websites. There is also one given below.

It is difficult to sit down for a short period before confession and remember a month's worth of sins. Therefore, you might consider making a short examination of conscience regularly (maybe even nightly) and making notes of your sins (a simple daily examination is included earlier in this book). Remember, however, not to beat yourself up. God loves you and wants to forgive you completely for all your sins. He wants you to love yourself, in spite of your sins, with the infinite love he bears for you.

Formal Examination of Conscience Based on the Ten Commandments

1. "I am the Lord your God, you shall have no other gods besides me."
    - Do I seek to love God with my whole heart, mind, and body?
    - Have I treated people, events, or things as more important than God?

- Have I tried to grow in the knowledge of God through daily prayer and scripture reading?
- Have I participated in superstitions or in the occult (including horoscopes, Ouija boards, channeling, tarot cards, or fortune-telling)?
- Have I taken time to teach my family about the ways of God and pray with them?

2. "You shall not take the name of the Lord your God in vain."
   - Have my words, actively or passively, put down God, the Church, or people?
   - Have I been hypocritical by adhering to a ritualistic observance while not actually living out my faith in practice?
   - Have I used profane language?
3. "Remember to keep holy the Sabbath day."
   - Do I go to Mass every Sunday (or Saturday vigil) and on holy days of obligation?
   - Do I avoid, when possible, work that impedes worship of God, joyful appreciation for the Lord's Day, and proper relaxation of mind and body?
   - Do I look for ways to spend time with family or in service of others on Sunday?
   - Do I attend Mass with the good intention to be attentive and prayerful?

- Do I receive the Holy Eucharist in a loving and respectful way, free from mortal (serious) sin?

4. "Honor your father and your mother."
   - Do I show my parents due respect and patience and maintain good communication with them where possible?
   - Do I seek to forgive my parents for past wrongs?
   - Have I respected those in legitimate authority?
5. "You shall not kill."
   - Have I harmed another through physical, verbal, or emotional means, including gossip or manipulation of any kind?
   - Am I angry, bitter, or resentful toward anyone?
   - Have I struck anyone in anger, intending to injure them?
   - Have I advocated for abortion, either through my opinions in conversation or by actively assisting someone in procuring an abortion?
   - Have I endangered myself or the life of another person through the taking of drugs or the abuse of alcohol or otherwise sought to injure myself?

6. "You shall not commit adultery."
   - Have I engaged in sexual activity outside of marriage?
   - Have I given my mind over to lustful thoughts or fantasies?
   - Have I viewed pornography or other sexually arousing images or content?
   - Have I acted impurely by myself or with others?
7. "You shall not steal."
   - Have I taken anything that did not belong to me?
   - Have I been dishonest in the payment of my taxes or in the submission of expense accounts in my business?
   - Have I wasted time and cheated my employer (including though purposeful laziness)?
   - Have I been extravagant in my manner of life, to the neglect of the poor of the world?
8. "You shall not bear false witness against your neighbor."
   - Have I gossiped, told lies, or embellished stories at the expense of another?
   - Have I purposefully injured the reputation of another?

- Have I condoned the prejudice and hatred toward people of another nationality, race, or religion?
- Have I been truthful in my words and actions?

9. "You shall not covet your neighbor's wife."
   - Have I honored my spouse with my full affection and exclusive love?
   - Have I sought the affections of another's spouse?
   - Have I engaged in or attempted to engage in marital infidelity?
10. "You shall not covet your neighbor's goods."
    - Am I content with my own abilities and possessions, or do I envy others whom I perceive to have that which I lack?
    - Do I wish ill upon those whom I perceive to have possessions or abilities that I lack?
    - Am I generous with that which I have, giving freely to the poor, the Church, those in need, and other good causes?

PROCEDURE IN THE CONFESSIONAL

Bless yourself with the Sign of the Cross, saying, "Bless me, Father, for I have sinned. It has been [length of time] since my last confession. I have committed the following sins." Then tell Jesus, through the priest, your sins. The priest then gives the necessary advice, assigns your penance, and asks you to say the Act of Contrition (below). Afterward, wait and listen as the priest grants you absolution, while you again make the Sign of the Cross. Then say, "Thank you, Father" and leave the confessional.

ACT OF CONTRITION

Say this prayer during the Sacrament of Reconciliation, after confessing your sins and prior to receiving absolution from the priest. You can also say it any time you want to express sorrow to God, such as after your nightly examination of conscience.

O my God,
I am heartily sorry for having offended thee,
and I detest all my sins because of thy just punishments,
but most of all because they offend thee, my God,
who art all good and deserving of all my love.
I firmly resolve, with the help of thy grace,
to sin no more and to avoid the near occasions of sin.
Amen.

AFTER LEAVING THE CONFESSIONAL

After you leave the confessional, take a moment in prayer. First, thank God for his love and mercy in dying on the cross so that the Blood of Jesus could wash you clean of guilt. Thank him for this great gift of the Sacrament of Reconciliation. Recognize that regardless of how you feel, *you are completely forgiven*, even for those sins that you could not remember and confess. Next, do the penance the priest gave you as soon as possible. It is a good practice, as well, to pray an Our Father or Hail Mary for the priest who has just heard your confession.

DEVOTIONS AND MISCELLANEOUS PRAYERS

"The Tradition of the Church proposes to the faithful certain rhythms of praying intended to nourish continual prayer" (*Catechism of the Catholic Church*, no. 2698). Draw upon this rich treasure. You will find many traditional prayers that speak the words of your heart.

A NOTE ON DEVOTION TO MARY

Mary possesses a unique and unparalleled role in creation. She is the Mother of God. Mary is "highly favored" (Lk 1:28), "most blessed among women" (Lk 1:42, KJV), and "all generations" are to call her "blessed" (Lk 1:48). Mary is venerated (not worshiped) as the example *par excellence* of purity, humility, obedience. She was given to us as our own mother in the words spoken by Jesus from the cross (see Jn 19:26). And from her example at the wedding feast of Cana, Mary bears the role of intercessor for all our needs (Jn 2:1–12).

Seek to live a life in relationship to Mary. Talk to her. Ask her to intercede for you when you are in most need. Receive her maternal love. Learn about and undertake devotions to Mary such as the Rosary, the Angelus, and the Regina Coeli (included in this book). Learn more about consecration to Jesus through Mary, First Saturdays devotion to the Immaculate Heart of Mary, and Marian apparitions (there are plenty of great books and information on the internet about these).

THE ROSARY

The Rosary is perhaps the most efficacious vehicle for personal sanctification and heavenly intercession. The pages of this guide could not begin to contain the list of canonized saints who attest to this fact. Mary herself, in her several apparitions, pleads with her beloved children to pray the Rosary.

In the Rosary, we contemplate different moments of Jesus' life on earth and in heaven, called mysteries. Each "decade" of the Rosary—one Our Father, ten Hail Marys, and a Glory Be—is dedicated to a particular mystery, and we group these mysteries into four sets: the Joyful Mysteries (Christ's childhood, traditionally prayed on Mondays and

Saturdays), the Luminous Mysteries (Christ's public ministry, traditionally prayed on Thursdays), the Sorrowful Mysteries (Christ's Passion, traditionally prayed on Tuesdays and Fridays), and the Glorious Mysteries (the Lord's Resurrection and the founding of the Church, traditionally prayed on Wednesdays and Sundays).

Contrary to some popular belief, the Rosary is not centered on Mary but squarely on Christ. This prayer prompts us to meditate on the most important aspects of Christ's saving work. Mary's role is that of our great intercessor and mediatrix. In all the words and actions attributed to Mary in the Bible (and thus in the Rosary), she points to Christ. She is "full of grace" because "the Lord is with" her (Lk 1:28). She is "blessed" because of the "fruit of [her] womb", Jesus (Lk 1:42). Jesus gives Mary to all of us as our mother through his words to Saint John, "Behold, your mother" (Jn 19:27). And Mary in turn says to us in her perfect example of obedience and love for him, "Do whatever he tells you" (Jn 2:5).

Make time to pray the Rosary. You can pray it while you're driving to work, exercising, waiting in line—whenever you have some quiet moments. Carry rosary beads or a rosary bracelet or ring with you. And if you forget to do that, you can use your fingers. (That is why God gave you ten.)

If you are married, try to find time to pray the Rosary with your wife. If you have children, pray the Rosary as a family. It's a great way to spend time together in the car.

The following illustration shows how to pray the Rosary, and the particular prayers follow.

THE APOSTLES' CREED

I believe in God, the Father Almighty,
Creator of heaven and earth,
and in Jesus Christ, his only Son, our Lord,
who was conceived by the Holy Spirit,
born of the Virgin Mary,
suffered under Pontius Pilate,
was crucified, died and was buried.
He descended into hell.
On the third day he rose again.
He ascended into heaven
and is seated at the right hand of the Father.
From thence he shall come to judge the living and the dead.
I believe in the Holy Spirit,
the holy Catholic Church,
the communion of saints,
the forgiveness of sins,
the resurrection of the body
and life everlasting. Amen.

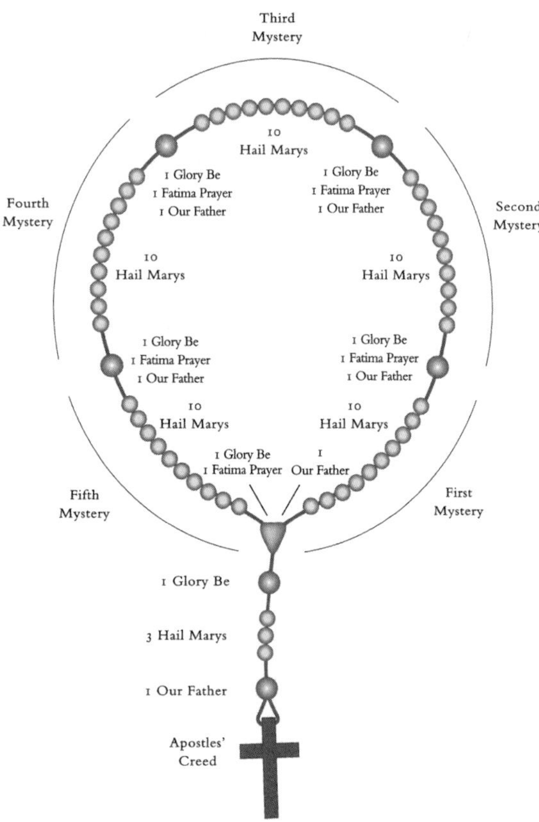
Third
Mystery
10
Hail Marys
1 Glory Be
1 Fatima Prayer
1 Our Father
1 Glory Be
1 Fatima Prayer
1 Our Father
Fourth
Mystery
Second
Mystery
10
Hail Marys
10
Hail Marys
1 Glory Be
1 Fatima Prayer
1 Our Father
1 Glory Be
1 Fatima Prayer
1 Our Father
10
Hail Marys
10
Hail Marys
1 Glory Be
1 Fatima Prayer
1
Our Father
Fifth
Mystery
First
Mystery
1 Glory Be
3 Hail Marys
1 Our Father
Apostles'
Creed

Our Father

Our Father, who art in heaven,
hallowed be thy name.
Thy kingdom come.
Thy will be done,
on earth as it is in heaven.
Give us this day our daily bread,
and forgive us our trespasses,
as we forgive those who trespass against us.
And lead us not into temptation,
but deliver us from evil.
Amen.

Hail Mary

Hail Mary, full of grace,
the Lord is with thee.
Blessed art thou among women,
and blessed is the fruit of thy womb,
Jesus.
Holy Mary, Mother of God,
pray for us sinners
now and at the hour of our death.
Amen.

Glory Be

Glory be to the Father,
and to the Son

and to the Holy Spirit,
as it was in the beginning, is now and ever shall be,
world without end.
Amen.

The Mysteries of the Rosary

Announce the mystery at the beginning of the decade, before the Our Father, and meditate on it while saying the ten Hail Marys. Each mystery is briefly explained below.

The Joyful Mysteries—Mondays and Saturdays

1. The Annunciation
   The angel Gabriel announces to Mary that she will conceive the Son of God.
2. The Visitation
   Mary, pregnant with Jesus, goes to her older cousin Elizabeth, in whose womb John the Baptist leaps for joy.
3. The Nativity
   Jesus is born in Bethlehem.
4. The Presentation of Jesus in the Temple
   Mary and Joseph bring the infant Jesus, a first-born son, to be dedicated to God at the Temple.

5. The Finding of Jesus in the Temple

    The twelve-year-old Jesus disappears for three days in Jerusalem, and his parents discover him teaching in the Temple.

The Luminous Mysteries—Thursdays

1. The Baptism of Jesus

    Jesus is baptized by John the Baptist in the river Jordan.

2. The Wedding Feast at Cana

    Jesus turns water into wine: his first public miracle.

3. The Preaching of the Kingdom

    Jesus goes about Israel preaching that the Kingdom of God is at hand.

4. The Transfiguration

    Jesus reveals his divine nature to Peter, James, and John on a mountain; Moses and Elijah appear before him, his appearance is transformed, and the voice of Father says, "This is my beloved Son; listen to him" (Mk 9:7).

5. The Institution of the Eucharist

    At the Last Supper, Jesus gives his disciples bread and wine, saying, "Take; this is my body" and "This is my blood of the covenant" (Mk 14:22, 24).

The Sorrowful Mysteries—Tuesdays and Fridays

1. Jesus' Agony in the Garden

   In the garden of Gethsemane, Jesus prays, "My Father, if it be possible, let this chalice pass from me; nevertheless, not as I will, but as you will" (Mt 26:39).
2. Jesus' Scourging at the Pillar

   Condemned by Pontius Pilate, Jesus is flogged by Roman soldiers.
3. The Crowning with Thorns

   To mock Jesus' kingship, soldiers place a crown of thorns on the Messiah's head.
4. Jesus Carries the Cross

   Christ bears the heavy cross from the praetorium to Golgotha, collapsing under the weight.
5. Jesus' Crucifixion and Death

   Jesus is nailed to the cross. The sky goes dark, and after hours of pain, Christ breathes his last.

The Glorious Mysteries—Wednesdays and Sundays

1. The Resurrection

   On the third day after his crucifixion, Jesus rises from the dead.
2. The Ascension

   Before the disciples' eyes, Jesus is taken up into heaven to sit at the right hand of God.

3. The Descent of the Holy Spirit (Pentecost)
The Holy Spirit comes down upon the disciples in the form of "tongues as of fire" (Acts 2:3).
4. The Assumption of Mary into Heaven
Mary, conceived without sin, is assumed body and soul into heaven—an event reported by Catholic tradition from ancient times.
5. The Crowning of Mary as Queen of Heaven and Earth
Mary takes her throne in heaven as Christ's Queen: "A great sign appeared in heaven, a woman clothed with the sun, with the moon under her feet, and on her head a crown of twelve stars" (Rev 12:1).

Fatima Prayer

O my Jesus, forgive us our sins
and save us from the fires of hell.
Lead all souls to heaven,
especially those who are in most need of thy mercy.

Hail, Holy Queen

Hail, Holy Queen,
Mother of Mercy,
our life, our sweetness, and our hope!
To thee do we cry, poor banished children of Eve;

to thee do we send up our sighs,
mourning and weeping in this valley of tears.
Turn then, most gracious advocate, thine eyes
of mercy toward us,
and after this our exile,
show unto us the blessed fruit of thy womb,
Jesus.
O clement, O loving, O sweet Virgin Mary!

℣: *Pray for us, O Holy Mother of God . . .*
℟: *That we may be made worthy of the promises*
of Christ.

Closing Prayer

Let us pray.
O God, whose only-begotten Son,
by his life, death and resurrection,
has purchased for us the rewards of
eternal life,
grant, we beseech thee,
that meditating upon these mysteries
of the Most Holy Rosary
of the Blessed Virgin Mary,
we may imitate what they contain
and obtain what they promise,
through the same Christ our Lord.
Amen.

THE ANGELUS

Traditionally, this prayer is prayed at noon every day, except from Easter until the Feast of the Ascension. If two people are praying it together, one should say the verse and the other the response. Both can then pray the Hail Mary together.

℣: *The angel of the Lord declared unto Mary.*
℟: *And she conceived by the Holy Spirit.*
Hail Mary

℣: *Behold, the handmaid of the Lord.*
℟: *Be it done unto me according to thy word.*
Hail Mary

℣: *And the Word was made flesh*
℟: *[bowing or genuflecting] and dwelt among us.*
Hail Mary

℣: *Pray for us, O holy Mother of God,*
℟: *that we may be made worthy of the promises of Christ.*

℣: *Let us pray.*
℟: *Pour forth, we beseech thee, O Lord, thy grace into our hearts, that we, to whom the incarnation*

of Christ, thy Son, was made known by the message of an angel, may by his Passion and Cross be brought to the glory of his resurrection, through the same Christ, our Lord. Amen.

THE REGINA COELI

Traditionally this prayer—"Queen of Heaven" in Latin—is said at noon every day between Easter and the Feast of Pentecost, instead of the Angelus.

Queen of Heaven, rejoice! Alleluia.
For he whom you did merit to bear, Alleluia,
has risen as he said. Alleluia.
Pray for us to God. Alleluia.

℣: *Rejoice and be glad, O Virgin Mary. Alleluia.*
℟: *For the Lord is truly risen. Alleluia.*

℣: *Let us pray.*
℟: *O God, who gave joy to the world through the resurrection of your Son, our Lord Jesus Christ, grant, we beseech you, that through the intercession of the Virgin Mary, his Mother, we may obtain the joys of everlasting life. Through the same Christ our Lord. Amen.*

PRAYERS TO SAINT JOSEPH

The Catholic Church reveres Saint Joseph as the model for all men and particularly for fathers and workers. This is the man God chose to be the foster father of his own Son, Jesus Christ. From the Bible we see Joseph's unfaltering obedience to God's will. He protected and tenderly cared for the Virgin Mary and the infant Jesus.

Joseph lived chastely, worked diligently, prayed fervently, and died well—in the presence of Jesus and the Blessed Mother. The great mystics teach us that Joseph's relative obscurity represents his choice of humility, so that the glory of Jesus would shine more brightly to all.

If you would be a true Christian man, pattern your life after Joseph, the patron saint of the Church, and constantly ask for his intercession on your behalf.

O Saint Joseph,
whose protection is so great, so strong,
so prompt before the throne of God,
I place in you all my interests and desires.
O Saint Joseph, do assist me by your powerful intercession
and obtain for me from your divine Son all spiritual
blessings

through Jesus Christ, our Lord;
so that having engaged here below your heavenly power,
I may offer my thanksgiving and homage to the most loving of fathers.
O Saint Joseph, I never weary of contemplating you and Jesus asleep in your arms.
I dare not approach while he reposes near your heart.
Embrace him in my name and kiss his fine head for me,
and ask him to return the kiss when I draw my dying breath.
Saint Joseph, patron of departing souls, pray for us.

Or:

O glorious Saint Joseph,
you are the obedient servant of our God,
the chaste spouse of the Virgin Mary,
the foster father of the Word Incarnate,
the protector of the Holy Family
and the model for all Christian men.
In the love you bear for the Divine Infant, intercede for me,
that my prayer might find favor before God's throne.

The Litany of Saint Joseph

Lord, have mercy on us.
Christ, have mercy on us.
Lord, have mercy on us.
Christ, hear us.
Christ, graciously hear us.
God, the Father of heaven, have mercy on us.
God the Son, Redeemer of the world, have mercy on us.
God the Holy Spirit, have mercy on us.
Holy Trinity, one God, have mercy on us.
Holy Mary, pray for us.
Holy Joseph, pray for us.
Noble son of the house of David, pray for us.
Light of the patriarchs, pray for us.
Husband of the Mother of God, pray for us.
Chaste guardian of the Virgin, pray for us.
Foster father of the Son of God, pray for us.
Diligent defender of Christ, pray for us.
Head of the Holy Family, pray for us.
Joseph most just, pray for us.
Joseph most chaste, pray for us.
Joseph most prudent, pray for us.
Joseph most valiant, pray for us.
Joseph most obedient, pray for us.
Joseph most faithful, pray for us.

Mirror of patience, pray for us.
Lover of poverty, pray for us.
Model of all who labor, pray for us.
Glory of family life, pray for us.
Protector of virgins, pray for us.
Pillar of families, pray for us.
Consolation of the afflicted, pray for us.
Hope of the sick, pray for us.
Patron of the dying, pray for us.
Terror of the demons, pray for us.
Protector of the holy Church, pray for us.
Lamb of God, you take away the sins of the world, have mercy on us.
Lamb of God, you take away the sins of the world, have mercy on us.
Lamb of God, you take away the sins of the world, have mercy on us.
O God, you were pleased to choose Saint Joseph
as the husband of Mary and the guardian of your Son.
Grant that as we venerate him as our protector on earth,
we may deserve to have him as our intercessor in heaven.
We ask this through Christ our Lord.
Amen.

Get out your rosary again to pray this chaplet. The illustration shows the prayers for each bead, which are listed below.

1. The Sign of the Cross
2. Opening Prayer

   A. [Optional]

   You expired, Jesus, but the source of life gushed forth for souls, and the ocean of mercy opened up for the whole world. O Fount of Life, unfathomable Divine Mercy, envelop the whole world and empty yourself out upon us.

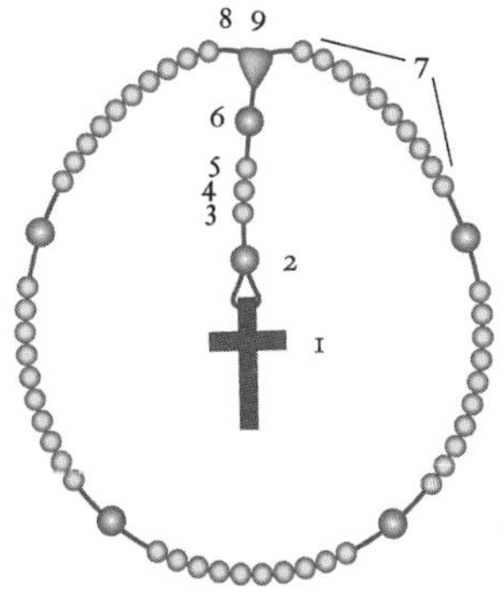

B. [Repeat three times]

O Blood and Water, which gushed forth from the Heart of Jesus as a fount of mercy for us, I trust in You!

3. Our Father
4. Hail Mary
5. Apostles' Creed
6. On each large bead, pray:

   Eternal Father, I offer you the Body and Blood, Soul and Divinity
   of your dearly Beloved Son, our Lord Jesus Christ,
   in atonement for our sins and those of the whole world.

7. On each of the ten small beads:

   For the sake of his sorrowful Passion,
   have mercy on us and on the whole world.

8. After five decades:

   Holy God, Holy Mighty One, Holy Immortal One,
   have mercy on us and on the whole world. [three times]
   Jesus, I trust in you! [three times]

9. Optional Closing Prayer:

   Eternal God, in whom mercy is endless and the treasury of compassion—inexhaustible, look kindly upon us and increase Your mercy in us, that in difficult moments we might not despair nor become despondent, but with great confidence submit ourselves to Your holy will, which is Love and Mercy itself.

THE LITANY OF HUMILITY

O Jesus, meek and humble of heart, hear me.
From the desire of being esteemed, deliver me, Jesus.
From the desire of being loved, deliver me, Jesus.
From the desire of being extolled, deliver me, Jesus.
From the desire of being honored, deliver me, Jesus.
From the desire of being praised, deliver me, Jesus.
From the desire of being preferred to others, deliver me, Jesus.
From the desire of being consulted, deliver me, Jesus.
From the desire of being approved, deliver me, Jesus.
From the fear of being humiliated, deliver me, Jesus.
From the fear of being despised, deliver me, Jesus.
From the fear of suffering rebukes, deliver me, Jesus.

From the fear of being calumniated, deliver me, Jesus.
From the fear of being forgotten, deliver me, Jesus.
From the fear of being ridiculed, deliver me, Jesus.
From the fear of being wronged, deliver me, Jesus.
From the fear of being suspected, deliver me, Jesus.
That others may be loved more than I, Jesus, grant me the grace to desire it.
That others may be esteemed more than I, Jesus, grant me the grace to desire it.
That in the opinion of the world, others may increase, and I may decrease, Jesus, grant me the grace to desire it.
That others may be chosen and I set aside, Jesus, grant me the grace to desire it.
That others may be praised and I unnoticed, Jesus, grant me the grace to desire it.
That others may be preferred to me in everything, Jesus, grant me the grace to desire it.
That others may become holier than I, provided that I may become as holy as I should, Jesus, grant me the grace to desire it.

RAFAEL CARDINAL MERRY DEL VAL

As Catholics, we believe that the Eucharist is the Body, Blood, Soul, and Divinity of Jesus Christ. When we look upon the host, we are literally looking upon God (although veiled in the appearance of mere bread). That the almighty God, Creator of all, would lower himself to become man—truly man—in order to suffer and die for us is mind-blowing. Yet, this is the truth. God exists both spiritually and physically in every tabernacle of the world.

It is a wonderful habit to stop in a church from time to time and pray before the tabernacle. An even better opportunity is the practice of Eucharistic adoration. Many churches will expose the Eucharist in a monstrance (usually a gold, cross-shaped holder with a glass compartment that holds a large host). This affords you the opportunity to gaze upon the very Body of Christ while praying.

Adoration is a time to meditate upon the mystery of God's incarnation—becoming man—and the life, teachings, and suffering, death, and resurrection of Jesus. It is an opportunity to praise God and to thank God. One might spend the time reading the Bible or some spiritual work. It can be a time to sit in God's presence; to talk to God and to listen to God.

One of the following prayers might be said before the Eucharist or tabernacle.

Spiritual Communion

Invite Jesus to dwell in you, really and fully.

I wish, my Lord,
to receive you with the purity, humility and devotion
with which your most holy Mother received you,
with the spirit and fervor of the saints.

TAUGHT TO SAINT JOSEMARÍA ESCRIVÁ
AS A CHILD BY A PRIEST

Anima Christi

Soul of Christ, sanctify me.
Body of Christ, save me.
Blood of Christ, inebriate me.
Water from Christ's side, wash me.
Passion of Christ, strengthen me.
O good Jesus, hear me.
Within thy wounds hide me.
Suffer me not to be separated from thee.
From the malicious enemy defend me.
In the hour of my death call me

and bid me come unto thee,
that I may praise thee with thy saints and with
thy angels
forever and ever.
Amen.

ANONYMOUS, FOURTEENTH CENTURY

O Jesus, Hidden God

O Jesus, hidden God, I cry to Thee;
O Jesus, hidden Light, I turn to Thee;
O Jesus, hidden Love, I run to Thee;
With all the strength I have I worship Thee;
With all the love I have I cling to Thee;
With all my soul I long to be with Thee;
And fear no more to fail, or fall from Thee.
O Jesus, deathless Love, who seekest me,
Thou who didst die for longing love of me,
thou King in all Thy beauty, come to me,
White-robed, blood-sprinkled Jesus, come to me,
and go no more, dear Lord, away from me. . . .
O sweetest Jesus, bring me home to Thee;
Free me, O dearest God, from all but Thee,
and break all chains that keep me back from Thee:
Call me, O thrilling Love; I follow Thee.
Thou art my All, and I love nought but Thee.
O hidden Love, who now art loving me;
O wounded Love, who once wast dead for me. . . .

O patient Love, who weariest not of me. . . .
O bear with me till I am lost in Thee;
O bear with me till I am found in Thee.

FATHER H. A. RAWES

PRAYER TO SAINT MICHAEL THE ARCHANGEL

Saint Michael the archangel,
defend us in battle.
Be our protection against the wickedness and snares of the devil.
May God rebuke him, we humbly pray,
and do thou, O prince of the heavenly host,
by the power of God,
cast into hell Satan and all evil spirits
who prowl about the world seeking the ruin of souls.

POPE LEO XIII

PRAYER TO THE HOLY SPIRIT

According to importance, this prayer should not be last in this guide. Perhaps it should even be the first, as the Holy Spirit is the key to all holiness. The Holy Spirit is our Advocate, our Comforter and the Giver of Life. The Holy Spirit is the "power source" of the Church and of our lives.

Call upon the Spirit constantly, and you will receive the insight you need, the strength you need, the comfort you need—everything you need!

O Holy Spirit,
Soul of my soul,
I adore you.
Enlighten, guide, strengthen and console me.
I promise to be submissive to all that you ask of me
and to accept all that you allow to happen to me.
Only, Holy Spirit, show me your will!

DÉSIRÉ JOSEPH CARDINAL MERCIER